D1258402

CAPE EDITIONS 33

General Editor: NATHANIEL TARN

Histoire Extra-ordinaire

ESSAY ON A DREAM
OF BAUDELAIRE'S

Michel Butor

Translated from the French by
Richard Howard

JONATHAN CAPE
THIRTY BEDFORD SQUARE
LONDON

First published in Great Britain 1969
by Jonathan Cape Ltd, 30 Bedford Square, London, wc1
Translated from the French *Histoire Extraordinaire*
© 1961 by Librairie Gallimard
Translation © 1969 by Jonathan Cape Ltd

SBN   Paperback   224 61664 1
      Hardback   224 61663 3

Condition of Sale

This book is sold subject to the condition that it shall not,
by way of trade or otherwise, be lent, re-sold, hired out,
or otherwise circulated without the publisher's prior
consent in any form of binding or cover than that in which
it is published and without a similar condition being imposed
on the subsequent purchaser.

Printed and bound in Great Britain
by Richard Clay (The Chaucer Press), Ltd
Bungay, Suffolk

Contents

To Jeanne's insulted beauty

I

TEXT

Thursday, March 13th, 1856

My dear friend,

Since dreams amuse you, here's one I'm sure you won't find disappointing. It's five in the morning, so the dream is quite fresh. Remember that it's only one of the thousand examples of the dreams I am beseiged by, and I needn't tell you that their utter singularity, their general character which is to be absolutely alien to my occupations or to my emotional experience, still leads me to believe that they are a hieroglyphic language to which I don't possess the key.

It was (in my dream) two or three in the morning, and I was walking alone through the streets. I meet Castille, who had, I think, several errands to run, and I tell him that I will accompany him and that I will take advantage of the carriage to do an errand of my own. So we take a carriage. I was considering it a *duty* to offer a book of mine that had just come out to the madam of a great brothel. Looking at my book, which I was holding in my hand, *it turned out to be* an obscene book, which accounted to me for the necessity of offering it to this woman. Besides, in my mind, this necessity was actually a pretext, an opportunity to fuck one of the girls of the brothel *en passant*, which implies that, if it were not for the necessity of presenting the book, I shouldn't have dared go into such a place.

I say nothing of all this to Castille, I get the carriage to stop at the brothel door, and I leave Castille in the carriage, promising myself not to keep him waiting long.

Immediately after ringing and going in, I realize that my p—— is hanging out of the fly of my un-buttoned trousers, and I consider it indecent to show myself this way, even in such a place. Moreover, feeling that my feet are soaking wet, I realize that I am *barefoot* and that I have walked through a puddle at the foot of the stairs. Bah! I tell myself, I'll wash them before fucking and before leaving the house. I go up-stairs. From this point on, the book is no longer an issue.

I find myself in a series of enormous, interconnecting halls – badly lit, their atmosphere melancholy and faded – like old cafés, old reading rooms, or dilapidated gaming houses. The girls, scattered through these enormous halls, are chatting with men, among whom I see schoolboys. I feel very sad and very intimidated; I am afraid my feet will be seen. I look down at them, I realize there is a shoe on *one* of them. Some time afterwards I discover there are shoes on both. I am suddenly aware that the walls of these enormous halls are decorated with many kinds of drawings, in frames. Not all are obscene. There are even architectural studies and Egyptian figures. Since I feel increasingly intimidated, and since I dare not approach a girl, I amuse myself by scrupulously examining the drawings.

In a secluded part of one of these halls, I find a very unusual series: drawings, miniatures, photographic prints in a crowd of tiny frames, representing brightly coloured birds with brilliant plumage, their eyes *alive*. Sometimes there are only halves of birds. Sometimes there are images of bizarre, monstrous, almost shape-less creatures, like meteorites. In a corner of each drawing, there is a note : this particular girl, aged , gave birth to this foetus in this particular year. And other notes of this kind.

It occurs to me that this kind of drawing is hardly likely to suggest love-making. Another thought I have is this : there is really only one newspaper in the world – *Le Siècle* – stupid enough to open a house of prostitution and install a kind of medical museum in it at the same time. In fact, I suddenly decide, it is *Le Siècle* which has raised the money for this brothel scheme, and the medical museum is explained by the paper's mania for *progress, science, dissemination of knowledge*. Then I reflect that modern stupidity and nonsense have their mysterious use, and that often what has been done for the worst, by a spiritual mechanism, turns out for the best.

I admire the exactness of this philosophic sense on my part. But among all these creatures, there is one that has lived. It is a monster born in the house and that stays eternally on a pedestal. Although alive, it is therefore part of the museum. It is not ugly. Its face is even pretty, very sunburnt, of an Eastern colour. There is a great deal of pink and green in it. It re-mains crouching, but in a strange, twisted position. There is also something blackish that winds several times round its limbs, like a thick serpent. I ask it what this is; it tells me that it is a monstrous appen-dage that comes out of its head, something elastic like rubber, and so long, so long, that if it rolled it round its head like a horse-tail, it would be much too heavy and quite impossible to carry; that consequent-ly the monster is obliged to carry it wound round its limbs, which, moreover, produces a more attractive effect. I talk with the monster for a long time. It tells me about its troubles and its disappointments. For several years now the curiosity of the public has obliged it to remain in this hall, on this pedestal. But its chief problem comes at mealtime. Being a living creature, it is obliged to take its meals with the girls of this establishment – to totter, rubber appendage and all, to the dining hall – where it must keep the thing coiled round itself or lay it like a bundle of rope on a chair, for if it were to trail on the floor, it would drag the monster's head back.

Moreover the monster is further obliged, tiny and squat as it is, to eat beside a tall, beautifully proportioned girl. It gives me all these explanations, however, in a voice without bitterness. I dare not touch it, but it interests me.

At this moment (this is no longer in the dream), my wife makes a noise with a piece of furniture in the room, which wakens me. I wake up exhausted, broken, my back, legs and hips aching. I suppose I was sleeping in the twisted position of the monster.

I have no idea whether all this will seem as funny to you as it does to me. Our good *Minet* would have great difficulty, I presume, finding a moral interpretation for it.

Yours warmly,
CH. BAUDELAIRE

2

SAFE KEEPING

(a) The recipient

A language to which he doesn't possess the key.

A language to which he gives us the keys.

Let us unfold one by one, gently, the fingers of this hand that is closed over its treasure.

Not that he wants to keep it for himself, of course – why would he write a letter so quickly? – but he wants to protect it until the last minute, wants to give it intact to someone who will be able to keep it intact, here Charles Asselineau, the man who will increasingly become his best friend, whom he will appoint the executor of his will, the guardian and protector of all he has written, who will fight to preserve its integrity, even against Madame Aupick.

The indiscreet, the ignorant must be kept from opening the envelopes too soon, scattering this gold dust.

(b) Strategies

Let us take note of this haste, since he himself emphasizes it.

Let us take note of the almost naive stratagems he resorts to for his protection; for if he proclaims that such a dream is 'utterly alien to his occupations or to his emotional experience', yet he is careful to specify at the end that he 'was sleeping in the twisted position of the monster'.

Similarly, when he presumes that 'our good *Minet* would have great difficulty finding a moral interpretation', he seems to forget that several paragraphs earlier, he had just found one himself:

'Then I reflect that modern stupidity and nonsense have their mysterious use, and that often what has been done for the worst, by a spiritual mechanism, turns out for the best. I admire the exactness of this philosophic sense on my part.'

He admires it so much that the following year, in the 'Notes nouvelles sur Edgar Poe' that will serve as a preface to the *Nouvelles Histoires extraordinaires*, he will take this passage from *The Imp of the Perverse*:

'We might, indeed, deem this perverseness a direct instigation of the arch-fiend, were it not occasionally known to operate in furtherance of good ...',

as a basis of the following paraphrase:

'This primal, irresistible force is natural Perversity, which causes man to be for ever both murderer and suicide, assassin and executioner; – for', he adds, with a remarkably Satanic subtlety, 'the impossibility of finding a rational motive to account for certain wicked and dangerous actions could lead us to consider them as the result of the Devil's suggestions, if experience and history did not teach us that God often derives from them the establishment of order and the punishment of rogues; – *after having made use of the same rogues as accomplices!* such is the word that slips, I admit, into my mind, like a hint as perfidious as it is inevitable.'

(c) The guarantee

Dreams play a considerable role in Baudelaire's work, but this is the only one we can date, the only one, so far as we know, that he thus transcribed immediately upon waking.

What a document to guide us to the heart of what was then taking shape within him, to enlighten us as to certain aspects of this work that concerns us so greatly, to help us resolve so many of its contradictions that still torment us!

Indeed I often marvel at the naivety of literary scholars, who generally exaggerate the significance of the unpublished works they turn up. Discovering great differences between opinions that the poet expressed in his published work and those afforded by certain of his letters, as regards Victor Hugo for instance, they declare him quite simply, without questioning themselves any further, to be sincere in the latter, disingenuous or expedient in the former, which would certainly have scandalized him to the highest degree.

How can we, if we are ever seriously concerned with writing, put on the same level these phrases scrupulously weighed, corrected many times over so that they may finally achieve, after all this effort, some degree of precision or probity, this painfully, laboriously won 'sincerity', this public confession by which an author commits himself, and those other phrases, rapidly flung down on a sheet of paper which itself is rapidly flung into the post-box so that it need not be re-read, intended to reproduce such and such an effect, on such and such a day, on such and such a person, and concerning which one often hopes, even manages to convince oneself, that this same person, several days later, has forgotten them: lies, if they are lies, nonsense sometimes, injustices, which one supposes will go no further,

or else, quite simply, out of caprice, in order to take a secret revenge, in fact, on the admiration one feels, on the difficulty one has had in expressing it, on the fact that to communicate it at all one has had to suppress a certain number of reservations which return in private, maliciously, but which one would never print.

Truly, it is only too easy, and pointless, many times over, to convict Baudelaire of bad faith in his correspondence; he didn't write these letters to us, and these defects are on the whole only the wrong side, the price of that prodigious effort of mental honesty which his entire work represents, surrounded by darkness and disorder.

As he said of Poe : 'a part of what today comprises our pleasure is what has killed him'; a part of what today comprises our consciousness is what has blinded him.

If he so quickly put this concretion of himself in such safe keeping, it is also to guarantee it against all his own weaknesses.

3

THE BOOK

(a) The occasion

'One of the thousand examples of the dreams I am besieged by.' But it is for this one alone that he breaks his routine, that he gets up at five in the morning to transcribe it fresh, to give it into the safe keeping of someone who he feels – he knows – will protect better than himself this mysterious link of his chain, this testimony which he divines is an essential document, a key to that general riddle which his entire work, and the entire work that is his life, will propose.

It therefore stands out against a whole series of other dreams, against a continuity of dreams oriented mostly around the same themes, corresponding to a fixed situation. What distinguishes it so strongly is that since the preceding dream, in other words since the preceding night, one element has intervened, transforming the *données* of the problem.

What was it then that happened on Wednesday, March 12th, 1856?

The *Histoires extraordinaires* of Edgar Poe, translated with a preface by Charles Baudelaire, was published by the house of Michel Lévy.

It was his first book; aside from work in newspapers and magazines, he had hitherto published only pamphlets.

'If it were not for the necessity of presenting the book, I shouldn't have dared go into such a place.'

(b) Predestination

What a treat for a psycho-analyst! But let us not translate too fast.

The sexual content here is subordinated to another, a literary content, so to speak. One of the chief virtues of this dream will in fact be to show us how these two realms are related to each other in the poet.

Instead of attempting to explain all the idiosyncrasies of his work by those of his erotic behaviour, would it not really be more interesting to show that the latter is somehow part of the former, is in many respects a consequence of his deepest conception of his own role, his primordial function as poet,

which he has accepted, which he has assumed, to which he has dedicated himself, which he has not chosen,

for the true poet, according to Baudelaire, cannot freely determine his condition; it is a 'diabolical Providence' which has 'prepared him for it from the cradle', has 'dedicated him to the altar', has '*consecrated* him, so to speak', as he declared in 1852, in his first major study of Edgar Poe, has 'damned' him as he will say in 1863, in *Le Peintre de la vie moderne*.

He doesn't even grant this 'predestined victim' the hope of avoiding this fate:

'Will the nightmare of *Les Ténèbres* (Gautier's poem, for which Baudelaire has always professed an unreserved admiration) always smother these chosen spirits? In vain they defend themselves, take every precaution, perfect their armour. Seal every exit, double-lock the door, caulk the windows. Oh, we've forgotten the keyhole; the Devil's already inside.'

And he specifies, in the second version of this study,

the very one that opens the book published on Wednesday, March 12th, 1856:

'In vain they struggle, in vain they conform to the world, its prudence and its guile; they will perfect their armour, seal every exit, hang mattresses over the windows against the projectiles of chance; but the Devil will get in through a keyhole; a perfection will be the defect in their armour, and a superlative quality the germ of their damnation.'

The only 'freedom' he concedes this predestined being is that of transforming this curse into a blessing, which is why it matters so much that the act of poetry should be voluntary, the functioning of a prosody should provoke inspiration, for poetry is liberation within this destiny, and the being who avoids this one avenue of escape is simply crushed; there will be no other way out for him.

Inversely, no one can *choose* damnation in order to become a poet; a chosen damnation is not damnation, and cannot produce salvation, since there would be other, much simpler means of escaping it. But if you cannot choose damnation, you can at least mimic it and profit by the advantages which the true poets sometimes obtain, and of which, naturally, your fraudulent popularity will deprive them.

This is the source of Baudelaire's strange hatred for Hégésippe Moreau, in whom, at first glance, one would have expected him to discover a brother, but in whom he denounces a counterfeit, a counterfeit of Poe, of Nerval, and of himself.

'For him, everything has turned out well; never was a spiritual fortune happier. His misery has been reckoned as work, the disorder of his life as misunderstood genius. He has strolled along, singing when he felt like singing. We know those sloth-abetting

21

theories, based solely on metaphors, which permit the poet to regard himself as a chattering, frivolous, irresponsible, uncapturable bird, shifting his domicile from one branch to another. Hégésippe Moreau was a spoiled child who didn't deserve to be spoiled.'

On the other hand, Nerval and Poe, in their true misery, were able to work 'in their own time it is true, in their own way, according to a more or less mysterious method, but active, industrious, utilizing their reveries or their meditations; in short, exercising their profession with gusto.'

(c) The time

'It was (in my dream) two or three in the morning, and I was walking alone through the streets.'

All the tales comprising the *Histoires extraordinaires* had already appeared serially in the paper *Le Pays*, like those which were to comprise the *Nouvelles Histoires extraordinaires* the year following. Behind the first book, out at last, the second is immediately silhouetted.

It is in the latter that 'L'Homme des foules' ('The Man of the Crowd') will appear, which Baudelaire in 1852 summarizes in this way:

'At other times we shall find pure fantasy, modelled on nature, and without explanation, in the manner of Hoffmann; the Man of the crowd ceaselessly immerses himself in the heart of the crowd; he swims ecstatically in the human ocean. When twilight descends, full of shadows and trembling lights, he flees the neighbourhoods that have gone to sleep and eagerly seeks those where the human substance is still intensely active. As the circle of light and life shrinks, he anxiously seeks its centre; like men in the days of the

Flood, he clings desperately to the last focal points of political agitation. And that is all. Is he a criminal horrified by solitude? Is he an imbecile who cannot endure himself?'

Eleven years later, in 1863, in *Le Peintre de la vie moderne*, here is what this summary will have become:

'Do you remember a scene (and it really is a scene!) described by the most powerful pen of the age and which is called 'The Man of the Crowd'? Behind the window of a coffee-house, a convalescent, delightedly staring at the crowd, mingles, in thought, with all the thoughts swarming around him. But lately escaped from the shadows of death, he joyously breathes in all the germs and effluvia of life; since he has been on the point of forgetting everything, he now remembers and ardently desires to remember everything. Finally, he dashes through this crowd seeking an unknown man whose countenance, momentarily glimpsed, has fascinated him. Curiosity has become a fatal, irresistible passion!'

We see that in the interval the focus of interest has shifted for Baudelaire from the second part of the tale to the first. In 1852, the Man of the crowd, for Baudelaire as for Poe, is the man one observes externally and condemns, but in 1863 he has become the narrator himself. These two characters who follow each other through the streets of London are actually one and the same. The second follows in the footsteps of the first, who is unaware of him, the first man is unknowingly the initiator, the guide of the second, as Poe will unknowingly have been Baudelaire's. Here, as in many other cases, the translator's interpretation considerably deepens the author's own awareness.

Two or three in the morning, in this tale, is the

moment when the Man of the crowd, unconscious of his follower, realizes that life is about to stop in the region of the city where he happens to be, that he is about to be left alone, and then takes a long and solitary walk to reach another neighbourhood, 'the most noisome quarter of London, where everything wore the worst impress of the most deplorable poverty, and of the most desperate crime', but where, at least, 'the sounds of human life revived by sure degrees' until the moment, almost at daybreak, when the two of them suddenly came to a 'blaze of light ... one of the huge suburban temples of Intemperance – one of the palaces of the fiend, Gin'.

(d) The passer-by

'I meet Castille ... '

He has met him at 'L'Esprit public', before 1848, at the period when he was most attracted by the crowd and by political gatherings. At a certain moment, Castille has been for him that Man of the crowd who guided him towards the unknown neighbourhoods of the city of Paris; it is Castille who in the dream unwittingly leads him towards one of the huge suburban temples of indecency, and he appears all the more appropriately here since he has helped Baudelaire promulgate his works by bringing him into contact with the publishers whom he knows.

(e) The carriage

'So we take a carriage.'

When he describes the carriages that Constantin Guys dashes off on paper, Baudelaire will make veritable beds out of them :

'At a fast trot, down a road striped with light and shadow, the carriage conveys the beauties lying as though in a gondola, indolent, vaguely listening to the flatteries murmured in their ears, and lazily giving themselves up to the breeze of the promenade.

'Fur or mousseline rises to their chins and overflows like a wave over the *portière*.'

This carriage is in a sense the great brothel that has come to meet him. He no longer has to proceed in dreadful solitude; the Man of the crowd, the solitary man of the crowd, has led him to his destination; and all the time that it has taken, the whole of this agonized walk through the night-time streets of the city, is abolished in the movement of this vehicle. The aspect of things, of people, is transformed.

'In whatever position it is thrown, at whatever gait it is driven, a carriage, like a ship, stamps movement with a mysterious and complex grace extremely difficult to capture in shorthand on paper. The pleasure the artist's eye takes in it derives, it seems, from the series of geometric figures which this object – already so complicated, whether ship or carriage – engenders in rapid succession through space.'

(f) *The promise*

'I was considering it a *duty* to offer a book of mine that had just come out to the madam of a great brothel.'

A letter to his mother, dated two days later, tells us that at the time of the dream he had as yet offered no one this book of his which had just come out, that he was waiting for copies to be able to send her one.

On Saturday he received three, one that he kept, I

suppose, or that he gave to his companion (his wife, in our text), Jeanne Duval, and two that he took to his legal guardian, Ancelle, one being for his mother, on the cover of which, he writes her, he has 'scribbled worthlessly' (what wouldn't I give to see that scribbling!).

So there is no doubt as to the identity of the 'madam'.

The gift of this book fulfils an old, old promise. In the pathetic letter of 1844, in which he begs his mother to spare him the humiliation of a legal guardian, he assured her that he was 'on the brink of a beginning of success, the eve of that day' that he had 'so often promised' her.

A few months later, the legal adviser imposed upon him, he announced to her:

'All I need is twelve days to finish something and sell it. If with a sacrifice of 60 francs, which represents 15 days of peace and quiet, you achieve the pleasure of seeing me give you at the end of the month the proofs of three books I have sold, which represents at least 1500 francs, and hearing me thank you from the depths of my heart, will you regret it? Naturally I wouldn't boast of such a tour de force if the said volumes had not been already under way for an eternity, so long that the paper has actually turned yellow ...'

Needless to add that by 1856 none of the three volumes anticipated had yet seen the light of day, and that occasional works like the Salons could hardly replace them, nor even La Fanfarlo, published as the fifteenth number of the first volume of Les Veillées littéraires illustrées, along with two texts by other authors.

This 'book' that he had so long intended to give

his mother exists at last; unable to give it to her at once, he gives it to her in his dream.

(g) *The transaction*

Baudelaire interpreted the humiliation of a legal guardian as a slur on his virility. He was already rebelling against his stepfather Aupick, whom he never agreed to call father, but only, in his greatest efforts at affection, his 'friend'; and here, in the person of Ancelle, a new substitute for that lost father whom he never mentions and whom he himself should have replaced, a new impostor was standing in his path.

The court decision drove him back into childhood.

He wrote to his mother, during this 'transaction':

' ... the eve of that day that I have so often promised you. It is just at this moment that you choose to *break my legs and arms* – for, as I have told you, I cannot bring myself to accept a *guardian* as something harmless, anodyne. I already suffer the effect being produced – and in this regard you have fallen into an even more serious error – which consists of thinking that it will be a stimulant. You can't imagine how I felt yesterday, the discouragement that buckled my legs when I saw that the matter was becoming serious'

(the use of the word *legs* or *feet* to designate the sexual organ is an extremely common 'Biblical metaphor'; our dream gives a splendid example of this displacement a few lines later)

'something like a sudden desire to send everything packing, to stop bothering with anything now, not even to go to M. Edm. Blanc to get my letter'

(a few lines below we learn what is involved:

'Monsieur Edmond Blanc has given me a very kind

letter with which I shall try to obtain something at the *Revue* this morning',

and a few days later, in a new letter, he informed her that he had indeed gone to the *Revue*, that he had been 'very kindly received' there, had suggested a 'book on painting', 'which they are waiting for', and on which he offered to 'work industriously',

but then, on this day, he virtually gave it up)

'telling myself calmly : what's the use, I no longer need to – all I can do now is to eat up like a good boy whatever she's willing to put in front of me',

which naturally brings us to the end of our dream :

'its chief problem comes at mealtime ... (it) is further obliged, tiny and squat as it is, to eat beside a tall, beautifully proportioned girl.'

Baudelaire supposes that if he published a work before 1844, he would have avoided the legal guardianship, that humiliation so great that it undermines his productive faculties themselves.

He will naturally regard the entire affair as a manoeuvre on the part of his mother, with the complicity of his stepfather, to keep him from continuing to write, to smother the reproaches, the accusations his poetry will necessarily contain. He hasn't published yet – so much the better! In the poem 'Bénédiction', number one of *Les Fleurs du Mal*, which is practically a 'life of the author', he tells the poet's mother :

Et je tordrai si bien cet arbre misérable,
Qu'il ne pourra pousser ses boutons empestés!

In finally giving his mother a book, Baudelaire takes his revenge. He recovers himself before the imposition of the legal guardianship, he cancels out its effects. They had tried to transform him into a child; he recovers his virility complete.

'If it were not for the necessity of presenting the book, I shouldn't have dared go into such a place.'

Only publication makes him adult and free.

(h) Laughter

What matters here is not the consummation of the sexual act, merely its possibility. He declares that, to his mind, this necessity of offering the book 'was actually a pretext, an opportunity to fuck one of the girls of the brothel, *en passant*,' (and not, as an over-hasty analyst would tend to persuade us, the madam); yet, once his recovered virility is made quite evident, it is no longer of great importance. Quite the contrary, he is increasingly intimidated, and dares not approach a girl; in fact, he is no longer interested in the girls, for this timidity will produce, upon awakening, no feeling of uneasiness; he is very proud of his dream, he finds it extremely funny.

I wonder if Asselineau found it as funny as Baudelaire did. What is the source of this laughter?

The article 'De l'essence du rire', published the year before, explains that laughter translates an impression of triumph:

'To take one of the most common examples in life, what is there so amusing about the spectacle of a man slipping and falling on ice or on the pavement, or stumbling over a kerb ... It is certain that if we consider this situation more carefully, we shall find a certain unconscious pride deep in the laugher's mind. That is the point of departure : It's not *me* that's falling; *I*'m walking properly; *my* footing is firm and assured ... '

Noting that 'the comic is a sign of superiority or of a belief in one's own superiority', and thereby considering the comic as essentially modern, he bases his remark on the fact that his contemporaries find comic the pagan figures which were not at all intended to produce laughter. He cites, in particular, a first draft of the little monster in our dream, 'the little Priapi with their curving tongues, their pointed ears, all cerebellum and phallus'.

Upon waking, Baudelaire laughs at the misfortune of his brother, his double, this little monster 'that has lived', this child that for years – until this very day – was himself, who totters when he walks.

But there is no cruelty in this laughter; imbued with pity, it is an example of what he calls the laughter occasioned by the grotesque:

'The fabulous creations, the beings whose justification cannot be derived from the code of common sense, often provoke in us a wild, excessive hilarity which may actually seem to tear us to pieces. Obviously we must distinguish here, where we are dealing with a higher degree … I mean that in this case laughter is the expression of the idea of superiority, no longer of man to man, but of man to nature.'

What provokes Baudelaire's laughter is therefore the idea of his superiority won at last over the little monster with which he was identified, and also the idea that he has thereby conquered what those around him took for granted as the laws of nature.

4

THE SHOES AND THE TROUSERS

(a) The case of the shoes

Let us take note here of the common French expression for marriage: 'to find a shoe to fit one's foot',

but a letter from Baudelaire to his mother, dated December 26th, 1853, will tell us a story of shoes that interests us all the more for being directly linked to the book in question, the *Histoires extraordinaires*, the gift and publication of which were already promised long since.

At this date, he had already published some examples of his work as a translator in various magazines: 'Révélation magnétique' ('Mesmeric Revelation') in 1848, 'La Philosophie de l'ameublement' ('Philosophy of Furniture') and 'Les Souvenirs de M. Auguste Bedloe' ('A Tale of the Ragged Mountains') in 1852, then 'Bérénice' and 'Le Puits et la Pendule' ('The Pit and the Pendulum') which will be part of the *Nouvelles Histoires extraordinaires*

(we know that at the time the distinction between the two volumes did not yet exist; the work which was to have appeared the following year under the imprint of Victor Lecou would certainly have included all the texts already translated, prefaced by the first study of 'Edgar Poe, his life and work'),

in 1853, 'Le Corbeau' ('The Raven'), 'Le Cœur révélateur' ('The Tell-tale Heart') and, in November – in other words, very shortly before this letter – 'Morella' and 'Le Chat noir' ('The Black Cat').

A letter of December 19th informs us that he has specially sent her these last three texts. It is obviously her remarks about them that make him exclaim :

'The same maternal fury which lately drove you to sending me certain grammatical notes on an author you have never read has now led you to suppose that all my troubles were due to my being deprived of rubber overshoes.'

Baudelaire has always been deeply concerned with his appearance. The fundamental evidence, which he will try to express through a whole series of theoretical elucidations that are at first sight contradictory, being that poetry implies a morality and that this morality is independent of the common morality, leads him, on the practical level, to dandyism; as a matter of fact, since true morality consists in making one's life the equivalent of a work of art, the most elementary application of this ideal, the prophetic sign of its realization, is to present oneself to others' eyes as a work of art oneself, to treat one's body as if it were a work of art, making clothes the frame :

> Comme un beau cadre ajoute à le peinture,
> Bien qu'elle soit d'un pinceau très vanté,
> Je ne sais quoi d'étrange et d'enchanté
> En l'isolant de l'immense nature,
> Ainsi bijoux, meubles, métaux, dorure,
> S'adaptaient juste à sa rare beauté;
> Rien n'offusquait sa parfaite clarté,
> Et tout semblait lui servir de bordure.

The notion that he could have neglected himself, treated his own body as a common object, scandalizes him :

'As for your fears regarding the *degradation* of my person in the state of poverty, I want you to know that all my life, in rags or in comfort, I have always devoted two hours to my toilet. Stop sullying your letters with such stupidities.'

The frame is quite moth-eaten, but the body is still framed.

Moth-eaten, threadbare, and if he expresses himself so violently, it is obviously because Madame Aupick divined what he had tried to hide from her,

'moreover, didn't you tell me – and it's the only phrase that really struck me – *Keep nothing from me*',

meaning that he had pawned his clothes, which he will admit a little later on, first as though inadvertently :

'if I had today a considerable sum – 100 francs, for instance – I would buy neither shoes nor shirts, I wouldn't visit a tailor, or even a pawnbroker',

then, much more explicitly :

'even supposing that my clothes were pawned and that I should have to buy others'.

As for the *extraordinary* offers he is unwilling to accept, it is beyond doubt that they concern purchases of new clothes, new shoes in particular, apparently with Madame Aupick's approval, since she would pay for them out of her own purse.

Not only, since the imposition of the legal guardianship, must he eat whatever she puts before him, he must also wear only the clothes she buys for him.

But he needs money for other things besides shoes, particularly with regard to a woman whom he has tried to consider as a second mother, although he had, he says, 'almost hated her' (the former, of course, in

C

Baudelaire, does not preclude the latter), whom he has sometimes been able to imagine playing for him the role of Maria Clemm, Edgar Poe's mother-in-law, for whom he had such a great admiration, on account of whom he envied the American writer so much, as is testified by the dedication which will appear at the head of the first instalment of the *Histoires extraordinaires* in *Le Pays* for July 25th, 1854, but which had perhaps already been prepared for the abortive edition of 1853 and which was surely prepared for the projected publication in *Le Moniteur*, which he announces to Poulet-Malassis in a letter written this same December –

'Today, it is not only the pleasure of discussing his beautiful works that possesses me, but also that of writing at their head the name of the woman who was always so kind and so gentle to him. As your own tenderness healed his wounds, he will embalm your name with his glory …

'I owed this public homage to a mother whose greatness and kindness honour the World of Letters as much as her son's marvellous creations. I should be infinitely happy if a straying beam of this charity which was the sun of his life could, across the seas that separate us, fall upon me, sickly and obscure as I am, and comfort me with its magnetic heat'

(upon the publication of this first instalment, he will complain bitterly to Madame Aupick about the printers' errors which disfigure the dedication he set such store upon),

a woman, Jeanne Duval's mother whom he proposes to a certain extent as a model to his own mother, because she has given him 'her last resources without a murmur, without a sigh, and *above all without advice*', to whom he must render a last 'obligatory duty', her exhumation and reburial.

'THAT will come before the shoes; moreover I am so accustomed to physical suffering, I know so well how to adjust two shirts under a ragged, wind-ridden jacket and trousers; I am so skilful at adapting straw or even paper soles to my gaping shoes, that I feel almost nothing but moral grievances. However, it must be admitted that I've reached the point where I no longer dare make sudden movements, or even walk too much for fear of damaging myself more.'

Madame Aupick sent him, through Ancelle, the money he requested for the purchase of a cemetery plot necessary for a proper interment, but, with regard to the clothes, she sent the legal guardian a kind of letter of credit to his own tailor, a downright piece of clumsiness or cruelty, thrusting Baudelaire still further into minority and dependence, confirming his humiliation.

'To go to one's tailor', he writes to her on December 31st, 'turned my stomach; aside from the fact that I had to *go* there, and that this was already a chore, since my state of destitution has kept me confined for over eight days ... I then had to display this poverty, of which you can have no idea, before the salesmen in the shop, appear to receive Monsieur Ancelle's *charity*, and exhibit this wretched slip of paper on the counter as I left. A little thing like that always revives the memory of all the affronts I have had to swallow.'

He wants to send back the letter of credit, but this is possible only with his mother's complicity, for meanwhile his sartorial problems have grown still worse. The pawnbroker with whom he has left a pair of trousers, a coat and a waistcoat has sold the last two items. To be able to keep away from Ancelle's tailor, he requires a little money at once to redeem the trousers, 'the most indispensable item', and, as for the shoes, to send out for a cobbler, the state of those he has on his feet being such that apparently he dares not go into a shop with them on. Perhaps they have even become literally unwearable, for Baudelaire adds, in the sentence describing his visit to the pawnbroker, that he wasn't expecting the 'evening thaw'. He must have gone home with his feet soaked.

Madame Aupick lets herself be moved to pity; she sends her son, by the bearer of his own letter, an answer and a note for Ancelle which Baudelaire does not find sufficiently clear and which he touches up a trifle to improve it.

'Good God!' he exclaims in confessing as much to her, 'how much diplomacy, how many efforts to dress oneself.'

He can thus indulge himself, for the new year, in shoes and recover his trousers without using the letter of credit.

He will thank her on January 3rd:

'It is a great delight not to have the wind at my backside and mud on my feet.'

(b) Revenge for dirty feet

Baudelaire supposes that if his book had appeared, he would have spared himself all such humiliation, in which he relives that of 1844.

'Your eternal, quite fair, but also very irrational reproaches about my book: *The book? Where is it? These articles? Where are they?'*

The gift of the work will therefore automatically put shoes on his feet, but there is something still more important, for the existence of this work will considerably diminish the shame attached to the dirty, wet and shoeless feet.

For Baudelaire, dandyism is actually only the prefiguration of the poetic state. In 1853, since the book has not yet appeared, despite his hopes and promises, he can testify to his moral elevation only by the intermediary of his costume, or more exactly by the care he takes of his person; his sartorial poverty therefore impugns him altogether. But the moment the book is there, clothes become secondary, and even the body as a motionless object offered to public view; what the book frames and costumes is the entire life of this body, a sum of actions and thoughts. The shoes were only an indication, and we have the proof.

Publication will therefore give him not only the audacity and the right to go into the great brothel, but also the right to go in even with his feet bare and dirty.

'Bah! I tell myself, I'll wash them before fucking and before leaving the house.'

What little shame still remains – for these girls, these men, these schoolboys do not yet know that the book has appeared, that he is entitled to go barefoot – will vanish with the shoes that suddenly appear, giving way to a juvenile timidity accompanied by an enormous sadness.

He recalls himself, of course, at the time of his first visit to brothels. The schoolboys he glimpses are himself before the imposition of the legal guardianship, just as the little monster is himself from that moment to this day. How many years wasted in this metamorphosis! But another reason for this sadness is the ever-present consequence of those first visits, that disease which he has communicated to the woman lying asleep beside him in his bed, and which will henceforth make him hesitate over all other women. We read in one of the notes for *Mon cœur mis à nu* :

'The day the young writer corrects his first proofs he is as proud as the schoolboy who has just caught his first dose of the clap.'

For he can never again 'innocently' enjoy with whores his newly regained virility. The appearance of the book will not restore his former health.

(c) *The case of the trousers*

As for the trousers, a much earlier letter shows that this 'most indispensable' object must have played a decisive role in the relations between Baudelaire and his stepfather.

In this letter, which we can date November 1842, he apologizes to his mother for not going to visit General Aupick at the École d'Application d'État-Major, pleading as an excuse 'his total lack of trousers and hat'.

Now the scholars assure us that such words cannot be taken literally, for Baudelaire had no sartorial difficulties in 1842. It was at this period, according to his legend, that he ordered twelve suits like Goethe's, and we know that he distinguishes himself by wearing trousers specially cut to his own design, made of kerseymere, and not tight-fitting.

General Aupick, we are told, was extremely strict about the proprieties. He must have considered 'indecent' the famous kerseymere trousers and forbidden his stepson to come into his house unless he was wearing some other costume.

The luxurious indecent trousers which distinguish him call attention to him as a dandy – that is, as consecrated to poetry, one might almost say as a 'novice' of poetry – keep him from entering his mother's house. Eleven years later, the indecency of his trousers, worn ragged by poverty, risk keeping him from going anywhere at all. Only his mother can then help him dress without renewing his humiliation, without making him receive these trousers from the hands of Ancelle, a substitute for General Aupick, who would then triumph over him.

Here is what he replied, in a letter whose exact date is unfortunately unknown, to an attempt at reconciliation:

'It is impossible for me to make myself as your husband would like me to be; consequently, it would be robbing him to live in his house any longer; and finally, I do not believe it is *decent* that I should be treated by him as he now seems to want to treat me.'

The revealing trousers in the dream, which distinguish him as an adult, are indeed an indecent pair 'even in such a place'; but Baudelaire is now content to note the mere fact of this indecency and be amused by it; it no longer forbids him to go into this great brothel where he was born.

He must have laughed like a child, without questioning himself as to the reasons for his laughter, in writing the word 'indecent', in underlining the word *barefoot*, for these are two ancient prohibitions victoriously transgressed, two barriers crossed, by a childlike laughter, to quote once again from the article 'De l'essence du rire', 'not entirely free of ambition' (nor of pride, nor of revenge) 'as is suitable for these bits of men, that is, these budding Satans'.

5

THE CLAP

(a) Madame Sabatier's ink-well

We read in *Le Peintre de la vie moderne*:

'Genius is only *childhood rediscovered* at will, childhood now endowed, in order to express itself, with virile organs, and with the analytic spirit that permits it to organize the mass of materials involuntarily accumulated.'

'Endowed with virile organs', this connection between virility and poetry is so strong that Baudelaire comes to consider the woman writer a quasi-impossibility. The esteem in which he holds Marceline Desbordes-Valmore is a paradox which he merely underlines without attempting to justify it:

'More than once hasn't one of your friends said to you, as you were confiding to him one of your tastes or one of your passions, "Now that's extraordinary, for it's in complete disagreement with your other passions and doctrines ..."

' ... Such is my case with regard to Madame Desbordes-Valmore ... '

As a matter of fact, he declares a few lines later, after listing several types of poetesses:

'Our eyes, enamoured of beauty, have never been able to accustom themselves to all these starched uglinesses, all these impious villainies (there are even poetesses of impiety), to all these sacrileges, pastiches of the male mind.'

When he wants to express the feelings of the poet in general, images borrowed from masculine sexuality come to his pen quite naturally. Hence, in *Le Peintre de la vie moderne*, he will even declare:

'I assert that inspiration has some relation to *congestion*, and that every sublime thought is accompanied by a nervous shock, of greater or lesser strength, which echoes even in the cerebellum.'

This masculine sexuality particularly expresses, proclaims poetic power by being the individual's means of distinguishing himself from others, of opposing himself to society, of scandalizing it; it is therefore chiefly an irregular sexuality which will be the poet's sign, eroticism rather than engendering, and the more it is a sign the more visible it is, the more clearly the individual bears the scars, the stigmata of his dealings.

The publicity of disease is much like a first draft of publication.

Thus the clap which the schoolboy 'wins' – the schoolboy Baudelaire – during one of his first visits to a brothel, has confirmed him in his poetic vocation.

But the close connection between poetry and virility forbids him to communicate this disease to a woman, since that would merely cause her to share in the curse without possessing the means of turning it into a blessing. It is Baudelaire's certainty of having contaminated Jeanne, of being the source of her infirmities, that has literally chained him to her, obliged him to become her protector.

'I do not want anyone', he explains to his mother on May 18th, 1854, 'to see a wife of mine, *poor, sick, and badly dressed*, who has been known to be beautiful, healthy and elegant.'

With Jeanne, the damage already done, things no

doubt proceeded without difficulty, but when in 1857 a partial realization of this dream, the gift of *Les Fleurs du Mal*, a book accused of indecency, will have opened Madame Sabatier's bedroom door to him, we know that once this victory was won, he took no advantage of it.

When we read in the letter of embarrassed explanation that he wrote to her the next day:

'We know (I particularly) that there are knots difficult to untie',

we must understand that he was in no condition to take her in charge, to adopt her, as he had adopted Jeanne, a step he would have inevitably taken if he had communicated his disease to her. He is forbidden to indulge in any brief love affair.

Later, to reassure Poulet-Malassis, diseased too but not a poet, he will declare 'that there is no man in better health than the man who has had the clap and been properly cured of it ... It is a veritable rejuvenation', and we can well understand how he may have considered his disease not as a rejuvenation but as a guarantee of youth; only, despite the disappearance of the symptoms, it was then impossible for him to believe himself completely and permanently cured, since the mere fact of his cohabitation with Jeanne (who, to all appearances, was not entirely recovered herself) placed him at least under the constant danger of a relapse.

Moreover, we need merely remark that in the letter of December 9th, 1852, to Madame Sabatier, the poem he sent her, 'A celle qui est trop gaie', ended with these three stanzas:

> Ainsi je voudrais, une nuit,
> Quand l'heure des voluptés sonne,

> Vers les splendeurs de ta personne,
> Comme un lâche, ramper sans bruit,
>
> Pour châtier ta chair joyeuse,
> Pour meurtrir ton sein pardonné,
> Et faire à ton flanc étonné
> Une blessure large et creuse,
>
> Et, délicieuse douceur !
> A travers ces lèvres nouvelles,
> Plus éclatantes et plus belles,
> T'infuser mon sang, ô ma sœur !

and that it is only from the first edition of *Les Fleurs du Mal* onwards, the one which in fact he has just sent her and which has opened her bedroom door to him, but which no doubt she hasn't read with all the attention he counted on, in which she has probably not yet sought out the poems written in her honour to check whether they had not undergone some transformation,

that this last strophe has become :

> Et, vertigineuse douceur !
> A travers ces lèvres nouvelles,
> Plus éclatantes et plus belles,
> T'infuser mon venin, ma sœur !

That the word *venin* ('taint') had at the time, in this context, a quite specific meaning is proved by the 'publisher's note' written by Baudelaire himself, upon the appearance of this censored poem in *Les Épaves*, with the intention of protecting Poulet-Malassis against a new censorship, a protection that was discovered to be quite inadequate :

'The judges believe they have discovered a meaning

43

that is both bloodthirsty and obscene in the last two stanzas. The seriousness of the group excluded such *mockeries*. But that *venin* signified spleen or melancholy was too simple an idea for these criminologists.

'May their syphilitic interpretation lie on their own consciences!'

It was too simple an idea for everyone, and certainly, for Baudelaire, it must have been too simple an idea for Madame Sabatier.

It remains true that this taint, this venom is in fact the vehicle of spleen and melancholy, and the vehicle of damnation. The coward who infects a healthy girl with his taint does her an irreparable injury, plunges her into a permanent disaster; it is an unforgivable crime, and it is just this cowardice that Baudelaire accuses himself of. But the victim who can do nothing about this disaster has the power to communicate it to someone else whom it may enrich. Hence the girl, the one who so to speak 'administers' the venereal disease, appears to Baudelaire as a kind of priestess, a sacred *persona*, and inspires in him an intense curiosity mixed with veneration.

Féli Gautier relates:

'Baudelaire sought out prostitutes for the pleasure of his eyes, the amusement of his imagination and his vagrant whims, for the grace of their forms and the elegance of their posture, for all that spirituality that the atmosphere of Woman produces, by superposition of images and suggestive persuasion. To drink down great draughts of perfume, sound, colour.'

Jacques Crépet recalls, quoting this passage, that Baudelaire's friends had nicknamed him the 'spiritualist'.

At the end of his life, he visits 'the girls' the way a bigot visits churches.

There are things it is easier to say in verse, and in particular by changing a word in proof, than aloud. Unable to bring himself not only to 'infect' Madame Sabatier with 'his taint', but even to explain clearly why he shunned her offers, Baudelaire will find a solution a month later in an action which is a veritable dream-come-true.

Since he hasn't been able to give her the 'venom' she desired, he will richly compensate for this lack by offering her the very thing of which the 'venom' is only an image, only a harbinger, a venom incomparably blacker, purer, whose blackness

Semble fourbi, clair, irisé,

in other words, ink.

Instead of what is merely one of the poet's attributes, she will have this other attribute, the classical emblem of the writer – the ink-well.

Here is the letter he sends her on September 25th, 1857:

'Beloved friend,

'Yesterday I did an enormously stupid thing. Knowing how fond you are of old-fashioned things, I have had my eye, for a long time, on an ink-well you might like. But I didn't dare send it to you. One of my friends told me he thought of acquiring it, and that made up my mind for me. But imagine my disappointment when I found a worn, battered, decrepit object, which had seemed so pretty in the shop-window.

'As for the piece of foolishness, here it is: I left the shopkeeper neither my card nor a note for you, so that the object must have turned up at your house in the most mysterious way: I am the guilty party. So suspect no one else. I realized my stupidity only this evening.

'I send you the affectionate sentiments of your devoted friend and servant,

'CH. BAUDELAIRE'

We can imagine Madame Sabatier's perplexity upon
the arrival of this ancient and anonymous ink-well.
But who can overlook the fact that this anonymity
links up exactly with that of the first poems sent,
the first of all in particular: 'A celle qui est trop
gaie'.

(b) Eroticism and poetry

In 'Les Paradis artificiels', Baudelaire will try to reach
poetry by defending drugs against bourgeois morality,
only to condemn them later as precarious and dangerous substitutes for that absolute drug which is
poetry, 'the only miracle over which God has granted
us rights'. We see another apology taking shape in his
mind which takes as its point of departure a still more
universal 'temptation', surrounded by a more intense
aura of scandal: he would reach poetry by using
eroticism as bait, as an image to be transcended.

From this point of view, the 'Choix de maximes
consolantes sur l'amour' ('Selection of consolatory
maxims on love'), which appeared in *Le Corsaire-Satan*
for March 1846, one of our author's first publications,
a text still marked with journalistic frivolity, would
hold a place comparable to that of the essay in 1851,
'Du vin et du haschisch comparés comme moyens de
muiltiplier l'individualité' ('On wine and hashish compared as means of multiplying individuality').

One of the notes for *Mon cœur mis à nu* sketches
the development I suggest:

'The more man cultivates the arts, the fewer erections he has.

'There appears an increasingly apparent divorce between the mind and the brute.

'Only the brute has good erections, and fucking is the lyricism of the people.'

'Fucking' is presented as an ersatz and inferior image of the poetic act.

6

LES LESBIENNES

(a) The dreadful consolation

In one of the most celebrated of his *Fusées-Suggestions*, originally and incorrectly published in the notes for *Mon cœur mis à nu*, Baudelaire selects Poe as his intercessor, along with Mariette, 'the generous servant-girl of whom you were jealous', and his father – the real one, the secret, sacred, betrayed father, named, I think, only one other time in all his literary remains, here too with Mariette :

'Every morning say my *prayer to God, reservoir of all strength and justice, to my father, to Mariette and to Poe*, as intercessors; may they grant me *the strength necessary* to accomplish all my duties, and allow my mother *a long enough life* to enjoy my transformation ... ',

but he had already given the American poet this title ten years earlier (since this *Fusée* dates from 1862), in his first major study in 1852, which ends with these words :

'I would readily say of him, and of a certain class of men, what the catechism says of our God : "He has greatly suffered for us."

'On his tomb might be written : "all of you who have eagerly sought to discover the laws of your being, who have aspired to the infinite, and whose repressed emotions have had to seek a dreadful consolation in the wine of debauchery, pray for him. Now his corporeal being, purified, floats among the beings

whose existence he glimpsed, pray for him who sees
and knows, he will intercede for you" ',

a passage that obviously foreshadows the splendid
and celebrated opening of 'Les Paradis artificiels' : 'Le
Goût de l'Infini' ('The Longing for the Infinite'), and,
in the perspective of that other apology for poetry
which would take eroticism as its point of departure
instead of drugs, refers us back to a whole group of
poems, first germ of *Les Fleurs du Mal*, already written
in 1846 (whatever corrections and revisions the poet
made in them later), so that he was in a position to
announce on the cover of his *Salon* of that year :

'*Les Lesbiennes*, poems by Baudelaire-Dufays, soon
to be published.'

(b) 'Femmes damnées'

Longing for the infinite, dreadful consolation, wine
of debauchery.

And in fact we find in 'Femmes damnées' :

Il en est, aux lueurs des résines croulantes,
Qui dans le creux muet des vieux antres païens
T'appellent au secours de leurs fièvres hurlantes,
Ô Bacchus, endormeur des remords anciens !

Ô vierges, ô démons, ô monstres, ô martyres,
De la réalité grands esprits contempteurs,
Chercheuses d'infini, dévotes et satyres,
Tantôt pleines de cris, tantôt pleines de pleurs,

Vous que dans votre enfer mon âme a poursuivies,
Pauvres sœurs, je vous aime autant que je vous
    plains,
Pour vos mornes douleurs, vos soifs inassouvies,
Et les urnes d'amour dont vos grands cœurs sont
    pleins !

D   49

In 'Delphine et Hippolyte', we see the 'powerful beauty ... voluptuously' savouring 'the wine of her victory', and the other exclaiming:

Je sens s'élargir dans mon être
Un abîme béant; cet abîme est mon cœur!

Brûlant comme un volcan, profond comme le vide!
Rien ne rassasiera ce monstre gémissant
Et ne rafraîchira la soif de l'Euménide
Qui, la torche à la main, le brûle jusqu'au sang.

The end of the poem, added, according to Poulet-Malassis, a few days before the 1857 publication of *Les Fleurs du Mal* as a precautionary measure, brings us to this last line:

Et fuyez l'infini que vous portez en vous!

(c) Mundus muliebris

The imposition of the legal guardianship in 1844 castrated Baudelaire not physically but morally. His organs are intact, of course, but they are only a sign, and henceforth a deceptive one. He is no longer a man, he is only a child or a woman. His majority has been taken from him.

This does not prevent him from desiring women, from sleeping with them, or at least with one of them, but when he does so he is a woman who desires a woman. Under his man's suit, he is a Lesbian.

In *La Fanfarlo*, his alter ego, Samuel Cramer, has published a volume of verse, *Les Orfraies* (*The Ospreys*), under the female pseudonym of Manuela de Monteverde.

When in *Les Paradis artificiels*, dedicated (under

cover of the initials J. G. F., which no one has yet been able to explain) without any possible doubt to Jeanne Duval, he describes his own hashish dreams, he will attribute them first to a young idler, then to a literary man ('and, in certain passages of his narrative, one may, I think, find the hints of a literary temperament'), and finally to a woman, 'a woman past her youth, inquisitive and excitable, and who, having yielded to a desire to make the poison's acquaintance, describes thus, for another lady, the most important of her visions',

a woman concerning whom he will explain himself, in the second part of the book, by commenting on de Quincey's delight at having had only sisters :

'Indeed, the men who have been brought up by women and among women do not quite resemble other men, even supposing an equality in temperament or in spiritual faculties. The attentions of nurses, maternal cajoleries, the playfulness of sisters, particularly of elder sisters, a sort of diminutive mother, transform, as they knead it, the masculine clay. The man who from infancy has been steeped in the sweet atmosphere of Woman, in the odour of her hands, of her breast, of her knees, of her hair, of her soft and diaphanous clothes,

> *Dulce balneum suavibus*
> *Unguentatum odoribus*

has thereby contracted a sensitivity of epidermis and a distinction of accent, a kind of hermaphroditism, without which the harshest and most virile genius remains, in relation to artistic perfection, an incomplete being. In other words, an early taste for the world of women, *mundus muliebris*, for all its shimmering, sparkling and perfumed apparatus, creates superior genius; and I am convinced that my highly intelligent lady reader will excuse the almost sensual form of my expressions, as she will approve and understand the purity of my thought.'

His highly intelligent lady reader (the epithet is quite astonishing, for neither his biographers nor Baudelaire himself have often applied it to her), Jeanne Lemer, alias Jeanne Prosper, alias Jeanne Duval, before becoming his adopted daughter, has been his elder sister, his diminutive mother.

The Latin quotation is taken from 'Franciscae meae laudes' in *Les Fleurs du Mal*, and the expression *mundus muliebris* will be repeated and commented on in a magnificent page of *Le Peintre de la vie moderne*:

'The artists who have particularly applied themselves to the study of this enigmatic being dote as much on the entire *mundus muliebris* as on woman herself. Woman is no doubt a light, a look, an invitation to happiness, a word sometimes; but she is above all a general harmony, not only in her passing and the movement of her limbs, but also in the mousselines, the gauzes, the vast and shimmering clouds of stuffs which she wraps about herself, and which are like the attributes and the pedestal of her divinity; in the metal and mineral which entwine her arms and her neck, which add their sparks to the fire of her eyes, or which tinkle gently at her ears ... '

In one of his notes, probably a plan for a tale:

'Even as a boy, the skirts, the silk, the perfumes, the knees of women',

which we find again in almost the same form in one of the *Fusées*:

'The early taste for women. I confused the smell of fur with the aroma of women. I remember ... After all, I loved my mother for her elegance. So I was a precocious dandy.'

Not only does he love women, he also loves all that they love.

In appearance, what could be more contradictory than this exaltation of the *mundus muliebris* ('woman is not only for the artist in general, and for M. G. in particular, the female of the human species. She is actually a divinity, a star which presides over all the conceptions of the male brain') throughout *Le Peintre de la vie moderne*, and the misogyny that explodes in so many notes for *Mon cœur mis à nu*, certainly written at the same period, that misogyny he attributed to Poe in the 1852 article:

'Another special characteristic of his literature is that it is entirely anti-feminine ... ',

than this affirmation of the artist's hermaphroditism and the fact that virility is the very sign of creative power!

(d) The disappointment

With regard to the misogynist notes for *Mon cœur mis à nu* and their contradiction in a text like *Le Peintre de la vie moderne*, it is obvious that we have here something parallel to the insulting notes about George Sand or Victor Hugo, and their contradiction in the public praise Baudelaire showers upon them.

These are the reactions of mood, the backwash of an admiration that would like to be more complete.

A certain insulting tone in Baudelaire – not the kind of pamphleteering eloquence and irony he uses to overwhelm Villemain, but the almost abject peevishness that grates through certain of his private papers – is always linked to a deep disappointment, apropos of which we feel that in his eyes the responsible party is only partly the person to whom the insult is addressed, for then it would be outright, obvious, even generous, and for which he himself feels responsible despite himself, so that he aims at himself as well as at the other person, his ostensible target.

He makes the phrase grate on purpose, for he is furious at having reached the point, even in this solitude, even in these letters or notes not at all intended to be published as they stand, of attacking what he is attacking.

To take revenge on his disappointment, he makes himself into a secret executioner, but since he knows perfectly well that the other person, his target, is not alone at fault, that his own incapacity to formulate the difficulties that these others will not help him with is also at fault, his own incapacity to vanquish the contradictions which undermine him and which these others reopen like old wounds; he takes revenge on himself as well for having become the executioner of others, by becoming an ignominious executioner, daubing his face with blood and assuming a harsh voice he is sure will be recognized, so that children will run away when he comes near.

Nothing is more characteristic in this regard than the *Argument du livre sur la Belgique*, in which he parades the very same stupidity, the very same vulgarity that he blames the Belgians for, that he cannot help blaming them for, when this can only be unfair if he considers the matter more lucidly. He does not forgive himself for not having found anything else in Belgium, and by the way in which he speaks voluntarily exposes himself to refutation. He pleads with his reader, the recipient of his letters or himself, to show him his mistakes, to correct, to challenge this judgment that is so manifestly warped.

(e) Travesties

A more careful reading of this passage of *Les Paradis artificiels* will show us how these two aspects – femininity, supervirility – far from excluding each other, are related. As a matter of fact, in this same sentence in which we are told that without this hermaphroditism genius remains incomplete, genius at its peak is characterized as 'the harshest and most virile genius'.

This is because for Baudelaire virility always means will, the power to achieve an intention, what has been decided on.

Woman makes of herself a work of art, but spontaneously, without having desired to do so; the dandy consciously makes himself into a work of art, but no more than externally; only the poet succeeds in making his very life into a work of art.

Hence the more intentional virility is, the more deliberate, the more conquered or, more exactly, reconquered, the more magnificent it will be. It must have been put to the test, and must be put to the test constantly, must emerge from a femininity that threatens to engulf it.

Achilles never declares himself more strongly as a virile hero than among the women's clothes he was wearing on Scyros, among the daughters of Lycomedon.

The *mundus muliebris* is thus the necessary theatre of the appearance of genius. The more voluminous the female garments, the more decisive the victory of the poet who tears them to shreds.

Hence we understand why the Lesbian becomes the very symbol of the apprentice poet, of the man who has not yet published. Publication will reveal this superior man hidden under a woman's dress and role.

In the fifth section of the *Salon de 1846*, Baudelaire, deploring the lack of any great erotic painting, dreams of an enormous 'museum of love, in which everything would have its place, from the untested tenderness of Saint Theresa to the serious debauches of the bored ages'. The only real work which he can suggest for such an exhibition is the following:

'Yet I remember one lithograph which expresses – without too much delicacy, unfortunately – one of the great truths of libertine love. A young man disguised as a woman and his mistress dressed as a man are sitting beside one another on a sofa – the kind of sofa you might suspect, the sofa of the furnished room and the one-night-stand hotel. The young woman is trying to lift her lover's skirts.'

(f) 'Sed non satiata'

Magically disguised as a woman, as though by an enchantment of the thousand and one nights, Baudelaire, in order to emerge from such a metamorphosis, requires this audacious woman's help; he needs her initiation.

In the only one of his letters to Jeanne that remains to us, dated December 17th, 1859 – that is, from the period when he was still working on *Les Paradis artificiels* – Baudelaire calls her 'my dear daughter' and, in his letters of the period to his mother, says he is playing the role of 'papa and guardian', of 'sister of charity and guardian' towards her. On the other hand, in the dedication to this work, he recalls the time when she wiped 'his sweat-drenched brow and *cooled his lips that were papery with fever*', watched over his nightmares and dissipated 'the dreadful slumber with a light and maternal hand'.

It is apparent that in the meantime relations have been reversed. She was a kind of mother; he is now a kind of father. She was an elder sister, a woman in a man's role, the one who showed the way.

A woman disguised as a man, a woman in a man's role. We read in the 'Choix de maximes consolantes sur l'amour':

'Never speak ill of great Nature, and if she has granted you a flat-chested mistress, say: "I possess a friend – with hips!" and go to the temple to render up thanks to the gods.'

The identification of this 'friend' is not at all dubious, for in 'Les Bijoux', a poem certainly conse-crated to Jeanne, we find this connection again:

Je croyais voir unis par un nouveau dessin
Les hanches de l'Antiope au buste d'un imberbe,
Tant sa taille faisait ressortir son bassin.

The Antiope in question is the magnificent Cor-reggio in the Louvre, which represents the daughter of Nyctaeus, King of Thebes, seduced in her sleep by Zeus in the form of a satyr. But the name Antiope ob-viously suggests to Baudelaire another much more famous heroine, the one for instance referred to in these lines of the murkiest tragedy of our classics:

Quels courages Vénus n'a-t-elle pas domptées?
Vous-même où seriez-vous, vous qui la combattez,
Si toujours Antiope à ses lois opposée
D'un pudique ardeur n'eût brûlé pour Thésée?

What is surprising about discovering in 'Delphine et Hippolyte' a Racinian echo? It is obviously from

Phèdre that this name comes. For Antiope, *this* Antiope, is not only the mother of a Hippolytus, but also the sister of a Hippolyta, queen of the Amazons.

In these 'Femmes damnées', it is of course Baudelaire who is Hippolyte, 'the child' dreaming

> aux caresses puissantes
> Qui levaient le rideau de sa jeune candeur.

It is evidently Jeanne who is Antiope or Delphine,

> Beauté forte à genoux devant la beauté frêle,

whose

> baisers sont légers comme ces éphémères
> Qui caressent le soir les grands lacs transparents.

As for the name Delphine, one of the stanzas makes it clear that it comes from the city of Delphi; she is the sibyl or pythoness, both oracle and guide in Hades:

> Delphine secouant sa crinière tragique,
> Et comme trépignant sur le trépied de fer,
> L'œil fatal, répondit d'une voix despotique:
> 'Qui donc devant l'amour ose parler d'enfer?'

Delphine-Jeanne offers Hippolyte-Baudelaire a dark mirror in which he studies his own vocation:

> Lesbos, terre des nuits chaudes et langoureuses,
> Qui font qu'à leurs miroirs, stérile volupté!
> Les filles aux yeux creux, de leurs corps amoureuses,
> Caressent les fruits mûrs de leur nubilité;
>
> ...
>
> Car Lesbos entre tous m'a choisi sur la terre
> Pour chanter le secret de ses vierges en fleurs,
> Et je fus dès l'enfance admis au noir mystère
> Des rires effrénés mêlés aux sombres pleurs...

In the sonnet 'Sed non satiata', whose very title announces the opening of *Les Paradis artificiels*, 'The Longing for the Infinite', Jeanne is explicitly compared to stimulants:

> Je préfère au constance, à l'opium, au nuits,
> L'élixir de ta bouche où l'amour se pavane ...

We shall find Racinian echoes throughout this poem:

> Par ces deux grands yeux noirs, soupiraux de ton
>   âme,
> Ô démon sans pitié! verse-moi moins de flamme;
> Je ne suis pas le Styx pour t'embrasser neuf fois,
>
> Hélas! et je ne puis, Mégère libertine,
> Pour briser ton courage et te mettre aux abois,
> Dans l'enfer de ton lit devenir Proserpine!

The name of Mégère reminds us of the verse from *Iphigénie*:

> Ô monstre que Mégère en ses flancs a porté!

and the name of Proserpine recalls Phèdre's declaration to Hippolyte:

> Je l'aime, non point tel que l'ont vu les enfers
> Volage adorateur de mille objets divers
> Qui va du dieu des morts déshonorer la couche ...

A most curious text, disclosed by Nadar and apparently dating from 1848, *Clergeon aux enfers*, gives us a singular paraphrase of this rape.

Clergeon, Nadar tells us, is the pseudonym of Songeon, a former pupil, along with Baudelaire and Nadar himself, at the Collège de Lyon, son of a general of the Empire, and eventually president of the Municipal Council of Paris.

Certain passages of this fantasy are quite closely related to our dream. As a matter of fact, Hell is here described as a great brothel. Clergeon, who is obviously also Baudelaire himself, 'goes in with a determined look, like timid men'. He asks to see the madam :

'He slides along by *anfractuosities known only to himself* and goes to wait for the Queen of Hell to appear at the *little door*.

'He follows her up the concealed staircase, and no sooner is he in her room than he tosses fifteen francs on to the dresser, a sum which the Devils who searched him when he came in forgot to take away from him.

' *"That's for you, my girl!"* he exclaims in a stentorian voice. "That's how a damned soul like myself can humiliate a Queen who betrays her husband."

'Proserpine, who hasn't seen such a bugger for six thousand years, tries to hang herself on the bell-pull.

'But Clergeon wastes no time; he will take advantage of his last seconds, dishonour Proserpine, screw her or know the reason why. He throws himself on top of her and plants his prick in her eye.'

Clergeon is a mock Theseus, Proserpine Madame Aupick. But in the sonnet 'Sed non satiata' it is Baudelaire himself who wants to become Proserpine, whereas 'Mégère libertine', the monster's mother, is here obviously Jeanne.

The enigmatic Latin title has provoked many commentaries; to understand it, we must realize that Baudelaire, in the last tercet, puts himself in the feminine.

Who is *non satiata*, unsatiated, here – is it actually Jeanne, whose coldness is deplored in so many other texts?

Et je chéris, ô bête implacable et cruelle!
Jusqu'à cette froideur par où tu m'es plus belle! ...

La froide majesté de la femme stérile ...

Tes yeux, où rien ne se révèle
De doux ni d'amer,
Sont deux bijoux froids où se mêle
L'or avec le fer ...

Obscurir la splendeur de tes froides prunelles ...

If there is anyone who is unsatiated here, it is certainly Baudelaire, it is he who so intensely regrets being unable to embrace her nine times, like the Styx.

Who is *lassata*, exhausted? Who has no more strength for a new embrace?

These tearless eyes, this masterful calm that drives him at bay, are indeed the sign that it is she – Jeanne, Antiope, Delphine – who is the mistress, the madam, that he is only the pupil and the slave, that he has not yet succeeded in reversing the roles, in gaining over this nocturnal deity the advantage of Theseus over the Queen of Hades.

How then can we fail to recognize Jeanne in this passage of the forty-second prose poem of *Le Spleen de Paris*, 'Portraits de maîtresses' :

'She was the illegitimate daughter of a prince. Beautiful, of course; otherwise, why should I have taken her? But she spoiled this great virtue by an unseemly and deformed ambition. She was a woman who always wanted to play the man. "You aren't a man! Ah! if I were a man! Of the two of us, I'm the one who's the man!" '

In the hell of their bed, the sexes were inverted.

61

(g) Jeanne's contamination

In the humiliation of the legal guardianship, Jeanne is the one who will show him the road back to his lost virility.

But this mirror, in which he greedily seeks the features of his future countenance that others had attempted to disperse and efface, now turns dim and, instead of reflecting the image of his glory, shows him nothing more than his condemnation.

The legal guardianship had castrated him; Jeanne's disease, affecting the very woman who was to 'intercede' for him, will repeat, will emphasize this punishment; he will forbid himself any dealings with other women; his desire will do without them.

In his notebook, he identifies the two things:

'Salvation is money, glory, security, the removal of the legal guardianship, Jeanne's life.'

Just after having drawn the latter's portrait in the 'Choix de maximes consolantes sur l'amour', 'a friend – with hips!', he begins talking about her disease. It is still 1846, there are only the first symptoms; he can still hope to evade the issue by irony, by paradox:

'Imagine your idol sick. Her beauty has vanished under the dreadful crust of smallpox, like foliage under the ice of winter. Still moved by her long sufferings and the fits of the disease, you gaze sadly at the ineffaceable stigmata on the beloved convalescent's body; suddenly you hear echoing in your ears a *dying* tune executed by the raving bow of Paganini, and this sympathetic tune speaks to you of yourself, seems to describe your whole inner poem of lost hopes. – Thenceforth the traces of smallpox will be a part of your happiness, and will always sing to your pitying eyes the mysterious tune of Paganini. Henceforth they will be not only an object of gentle sympathy, but even of physical pleasure, if you are one of those sensitive spirits for whom beauty is above all the *promise* of happiness. It is, then, particularly the association of ideas that inspires love for ugly women; for if your pockmarked mistress betrays you, you risk being unable to console yourself save with a pock-marked woman.'

When things grow worse, Baudelaire will no longer be able to continue in this tone. In a late fragment, he describes the end of the story thus:

'The voluptuary, after many hesitations, exorcizes his savagery in charity. What kind of misery can convert him? The disease of his former accomplice. Struggle between egoism, pity and remorse. His mistress (now his daughter) initiates him into the sentiments of paternity. – Remorse : – who knows if he is not the author of the evil?'

7

LES LIMBES

(a) Fourier

Once Baudelaire is faced with this confirmation of the verdict, Jeanne can do nothing more for him; he requires another creative mirror, which he will find in the crowd, during the 1848 revolution.

We know what transformations this revolution and its failure in 1851 produced in Baudelaire's theoretic systematizations.

Three periods are thus defined, which correspond not only to three aesthetics, but to three titles for the poems (*Les Lesbiennes, Les Limbes, Les Fleurs du Mal*), and, in the author's psychological life, to three successive intercessors: Jeanne, the crowd, and Edgar Poe.

These divisions are so marked that Baudelaire will no longer succeed in recognizing himself in the man he was earlier. He will try to deny his past by declaring that he has *always* thought in a certain way, that he has *never* valued this or that. This happens, for instance, in the case of Charles Fourier.

In a letter to Alphonse Toussenel that is extremely important for the interpretation of our dream, written a month and a half before the latter, on January 21st, 1856, he proclaims:

'After all – what do you owe *Fourier?* Nothing, or very little.'

(One almost wishes to reply: 'and then what?' as the dog said to the wolf in the fable.)

'Without Fourier, you would have been what you are. *L'homme raisonnable* hasn't waited until Fourier appeared on earth to understand that Nature is a *word*, an allegory, a mould, a *form*, if you like. We know that, and it isn't from Fourier that we know it – we know it by our own intuitions, and from the poets.'

A few years later, in 1861, in his carefully weighed article on Victor Hugo, he will modify this judgment by important nuances:

'Then came Fourier, all too pompously, to reveal the mysteries of *analogy*. I don't deny the value of some of his particular discoveries, although I believe that his mind was too fond of material exactitude not to commit errors and to achieve the moral certainty of intuition. He might, just as valuably, have revealed to us the excellent poets by whom a reading humanity is educated as much as by the contemplation of nature.'

We see that before recognizing his own thought in Poe's, Baudelaire had recognized it, to a certain degree, in Fourier's. In 1843 he had proposed an article to *La Démocratie pacifique*, the journal of Victor Considérant, one of the most active disciples of the socialist theoretician.

(b) 'Spleen'

The reference to Fourier reveals the profound relationship of the first two titles of the collection, so different at first glance: *Les Lesbiennes, Les Limbes*.

Indeed, the author of *Le Nouveau Monde industriel* gives the name 'limbique' to the civilization in which he finds himself, and which must be replaced by an organization of society that he calls 'harmonienne'. Limbo, in the Catholic tradition, is the place of

E

waiting, the Hades of the credo where the just of the old dispensation waited for the Saviour to open the gates of paradise to them, where, according to Dante, the just of pagan antiquity, who did not expect the Messiah on earth, are condemned to wait for ever :

Senza speme, vivemo in disio.

On April 9th, 1851, Baudelaire publishes in *Le Messager de l'Assemblée* a series of eleven poems under the title *Les Limbes* and announces the forthcoming publication of the collection 'intended to trace the history of the spiritual agitations of modern youth'. Three of them are entitled 'Spleen' :

Dans une terre grasse et pleine d'escargots ...
(in *Les Fleurs du Mal*, 'Le Mort joyeux'),

Il est amer et doux, pendant les nuits d'hiver ...
(in *Les Fleurs du Mal*, 'La Cloche fêlée'),

and the only one of the four which will bear this title in *Les Fleurs du Mal*.

Pluviôse irrité contre la vie entière ...
(in *Les Fleurs du Mal*, 'vie' will become 'ville').

Another :

J'implore ta pitié, Toi, l'unique que j'aime ...

called 'La Béatrice', will be entitled 'Le Spleen' in *La Revue des Deux Mondes* in 1855, before becoming 'De profundis clamavi'. Spleen is therefore the characteristic sentiment of this waiting.

So just as the publication of the book *Les Lesbiennes*, revealing under his women's clothes the poet's superb virility, must consecrate the abolition, the transcendence of the state described in them, so the publication of the book *Les Limbes* must contribute to the abolition of this 'limbique' society whose young people it describes.

At the time, the political significance of such a title was obvious. We read in a contemporary critic:

'Today we see a book of poems announced for publication with the title *Les Limbes*. These are no doubt socialist verses.'

Consequently, once the revolutionary hopes of 1848 were definitely extinguished by the election of Louis-Napoléon Bonaparte to the presidency, Baudelaire, discouraged, will write to his mother on August 30th, 1851:

'My book of poems? I know that a few years ago it would have been enough to make a man's reputation. It would have caused one hell of a row. But to-day, conditions, circumstances, everything is changed.'

(c) *The erotic power of the crowd*

It was the 1848 rebellion that had enabled him to discover in the crowd that instructive mirror which he needed, and when, under the Second Empire, he will have adopted, in disappointed reaction, certain aristocratic ideas, his earlier attitude will seem incomprehensible to him. He will question himself many times on this subject.

Hence, in one of the notes for *Mon cœur mis à nu*:

'My intoxication in 1848.

'What was the nature of this intoxication? The taste for revenge. The natural pleasure in destruction. Literary intoxication; memories of my reading ... '

In another:

'Intoxication with humanity; great picture to paint;

'In the light of charity;

'In the light of licentiousness;

'In the light of literature, or of the actor.'

The latter will be superbly developed in *Le Peintre de la vie moderne*, and in one of the *Petits poèmes en prose*.

In *L'Homme des foules*, Baudelaire recognized this temptation, this erotic attraction of the crowd, but whereas Poe concluded his narrative with a flat condemnation, Baudelaire hailed in himself this 'genius of profound crime', and in the summary he gives of this tale in his 1852 study we sense that the two questions commenting on it concern him specifically, are linked to this new condemnation which the coup d'état of December 2nd, 1851, signified for him:

'Like the men of the flood, he clings desperately to the last focal points of political agitation. And that is all. Is he a criminal horrified by solitude? Is he an imbecile who cannot endure himself?'

The expression 'political agitation' to designate this enticing crowd is of course not to be found in Poe.

In *Le Peintre de la vie moderne*, Baudelaire will insist on the fact that for Constantin Guys this crowd is actually a woman:

'His passion and his profession is to *marry the crowd*. For the perfect *flâneur*, for the impassioned observer, it is an enormous delight to seek one's home in number, in undulation, in movement, in the fugitive and the infinite ... The observer is a *prince* who savours his incognito everywhere. The admirer of life makes the world into his family, as the admirer of the fair sex makes all the beauties found, findable and unfindable into his; as the admirer of paintings lives in the enchanted society of dreams on canvas. Thus the lover of universal life enters into the crowd as into an immense Leyden jar',

which he will put to his own purposes in the prose-poem 'Les Foules' :

'It is not given to everyone to bathe in multitudes : to take one's pleasure in the crowd is an art; and only he can indulge in a debauch of vitality, at the expense of the human race, upon whom some fairy has in his cradle bestowed the love of disguise and concealment, the hatred of home and the passion for travel.

'Multitude, solitude : equal terms, convertible by the active and potent poet. A man who cannot populate his solitude cannot be alone in a bustling crowd.

'The poet enjoys the incomparable privilege of being able to be himself and anyone else as he chooses. Like souls wandering in search of a body, he enters, when he wishes, into each man's character. For himself alone, everything is empty; and if certain places appear to be closed to him, it is because in his eyes they are not worth the trouble of being visited.

'The solitary and reflective wanderer derives a singular intoxication from this universal communion. The man who easily weds the crowd experiences feverish pleasures which will for ever be alien to the egoist, sealed like a strong-box, and the idler, confined like a mollusc. He adopts every profession as his own, every joy and every sorrow that circumstances offer him.

'What men call love is so slight, so restricted, and so weak, compared to this ineffable orgy, this sacred prostitution of the soul that abandons itself completely – poetry and charity – to the unexpected which reveals itself to the passing stranger.

'It is sometimes good to teach the fortunate of this

world, even if only to humiliate their stupid pride for a moment, that there are fortunes superior to theirs, greater, and more refined. Founders of colonies, shepherds of peoples, missionaries exiled at the ends of the earth, no doubt know something of these mysterious intoxications; and at the heart of the huge family that their genius has created for itself they must sometimes laugh at those who pity them for their restless fortunes and their chaste lives.'

(d) Pierre Dupont

We see that the crowd as a whole, in its explosion, becomes a pythoness, a Megaera, much more powerful than Jeanne.

It is the crowd Baudelaire must obey, must imitate; it is the crowd that will give him the strength to finish and finally publish a book.

After this upheaval, his earlier dandyism seems to him as distant, as destroyed, as his socialism will seem after 1852.

We know that the great sign of this conversion is the article for the twentieth number of Pierre Dupont's *Chants et Chansons* in 1851, in which we can see very specifically how the crowd in revolt can play the role of instructor :

'I have just re-read carefully Pierre Dupont's *Chants et Chansons*, and I remain convinced that this new poet's success is a serious event, not so much for his own value, which none the less is extremely high, as for the public sentiments of which this poetry is the symptom, and of which Pierre Dupont has made himself the echo.'

What he admires in him, as in Auguste Barbier, is that he has been able to marry the crowd; and if we compare this text to the 1861 articles devoted to these two poets, we shall see that his opinion about the latter has changed much less than we might have been led to expect by the enormous reversal apparent in his aesthetic and political theories which has occurred in the interim. The ideas of the Pierre Dupont article, despite everything that contradicts them so violently on the surface, remain constantly subjacent.

Hence, when we read in *Le Peintre de la vie moderne*, apropos of the artist as man of the crowd:

'One might also compare him to a mirror as enormous as this crowd; to a kaleidoscope endowed with consciousness, which, at each of its movements, represents the multiform life, the moving grace of all the elements of life. It is a *self* always athirst for the *non-self*, which at every moment renders and expresses it in images more vivid than life itself, which is for ever unstable and fugitive',

we recognise a magnificent resurgence of the tone which was expressed in this passage of the Dupont article:

'I prefer the poet who puts himself in permanent communication with the men of his time and exchanges with them thoughts and sentiments translated in a noble and adequately correct language. The poet, placed on one of the points of humanity's circumference, echoes on the same line, in more melodious vibrations, the human thought transmitted to him; every true poet must be an incarnation...'

The article's close reveals quite clearly the programme that Baudelaire is drawing up for himself. Pierre Dupont is not the initiator, he is only the first disciple, the first to have understood, in his *Chant des ouvriers*, the lesson of this crowd that Baudelaire henceforth wishes to consider as his only true mistress:

'It will be to the eternal honour of Pierre Dupont to have broken down the door first. Axe in hand, he has severed the chains holding back the fortress drawbridge; now a truly popular poetry can escape.

'Great imprecations, deep sighs of hope, shouts of boundless encouragement are beginning to fill every breast. All this will become a book, will become poetry and song, whatever the resistance.

'What a great destiny poetry has before it! Joyous or grieving, it for ever bears within it the divine utopian character. It ceaselessly contradicts the state of fact, almost to the point of no longer existing. In the dungeon, it becomes revolt; at the hospital window, it is the ardent hope of health; in the shabby and filthy attic, it decks itself out like a fairy of luxury and elegance; not only does it bear witness, it makes reparation. Everywhere, it is the negation of iniquity.

'Advance into the future singing, providential poet. Your songs are the luminous tracing of the people's hopes and convictions!'

This *Chant des ouvriers* will be recommended to our admiration again in the article of 1861, with expressions that betray how much *déception* enters into it – in the English sense of 'ruse' as well as the French one of 'disappointment' – in a number of the theories Baudelaire will have adopted by then:

'However much of a rhetorician one must be, however much of one I am myself, and proud as I am to be so, why should I blush to admit that I was deeply moved? ...

'Was this song one of those volatile atoms floating in the atmosphere whose agglomeration becomes a storm, a tempest, an event? Was it one of those pre-

monitory symptoms clairvoyant men saw in considerable numbers in the intellectual atmosphere of France
at the time? I don't know; the fact of the matter is,
however, that, shortly after, this sounding hymn was
admirably adapted to a generalized revolution in
politics and the applications of politics. It became,
almost at once, the rallying cry of the disinherited
classes.'

(e) The contamination of the crowd

But this new mirror, too, will tarnish, and no longer
afford Baudelaire an image of his glory, but instead
that of his punishment. The Second Republic, far from
progressing, will turn reactionary. The popular
triumphs will be succeeded by abasement, repression.
He will interpret the December 2nd coup d'État as an
objective condemnation of his own attitude, a
new confirmation, after Jeanne's sickness, of what
the imposition of the legal guardianship had produced.

The crowd can no longer serve him as intercessor;
on the contrary he will wonder whether, just as he is
responsible for his mistress's disease, he hasn't, as an
ex-republican, in part provoked this humiliation
suffered by the crowd.

In a late note, connected with the *Argument du livre
sur la Belgique*, he will write :

'We all have the republican spirit in our veins, like
syphilis in our bones – we are democratized and ven-
erealized.'

Love and intense curiosity for the crowd are essential to the poet, a much more certain sign of his vocation than syphilis, but, just as he has no right to
communicate his disease to a woman for whom it will

be only a curse, so he has no right to commit the people, by a socialist prediction of whatever kind, to uprisings which produce in the last resort only an aggravation of the bourgeois tyranny; hence the extraordinary about-face of his political opinions, his proclaimed adherence to the doctrines of Joseph de Maistre.

Consequently we see that the declarations in the *Journaux intimes* (as they are deceptively called today) about *the people* are exactly parallel to those concerning women, and that they must receive the same interpretation.

(f) *The coup d'État*

This about-face occurred with astonishing rapidity. It begins between the writing of the article on Pierre Dupont and its publication. It is completed between the composition of the article on 'L'École païenne' and its appearance.

On August 30th, 1851, when he sends his mother the article on Pierre Dupont, he is already taking exception to it:

'Since I want to keep you informed of all I do, I'm sending you a little brochure which was generously paid for and which you will read only because it is by me, for I attach no importance to it otherwise.' It is in this same letter that he announces his discouragement regarding *Les Limbes*.

Henceforth he lives in the expectation of catastrophe, watches for the symptoms of the disease.

In one of the pages called *Fusées-suggestions*, we read:

'They say I am thirty; but if I've lived three minutes in one, am I not ninety?', which implies, as the first critics have pointed out, the date 1851, for it is difficult to suppose that Baudelaire, as Jacques Crépet suggests, had said 'thirty and ninety the way he would have said twenty and sixty', since, in a letter to his mother dated December 9th, 1851, but which we must logically consider as being written on January 9th of the same year, he declared:

'I am going to be *thirty* in just three months. This provokes me to many reflections whose nature it is easy to guess',

and since he returns to precisely this theme in this letter of August 30th, 1851:

'But at thirty, Balzac had for several years been accustomed to permanent labour, and hitherto I have only debts and projects in common with him.'

We are therefore obliged to date the anti-progressive note which precedes this thought in the *Fusée* at the end of 1851 or the first months of 1852:

'What is more absurd than Progress, since man, as is proved by daily examples, is always the same and like unto man, that is, always in the savage state! What are dangers of forest and prairie compared to the daily shocks and conflicts of civilization? Whether man cheats his dupe on the boulevard, or seizes his prey in the trackless wilderness, is he not man eternal, that is, the most perfect animal of prey?',

a text that we must obviously compare with this note for *Mon cœur mis à nu*, in which Baudelaire tries to comprehend, after the fact, his development at the time:

'My intoxication in 1848.

'What was the nature of this intoxication? The taste for revenge. The *natural* pleasure in destruction. Literary intoxication: memories of my reading.

'May 15th – Still the desire for destruction. Legitimate desire, if whatever is natural is legitimate.

'The horrors of June. Madness of the people, madness of the bourgeoisie. Natural love of crime.

'My rage over the coup d'État. How many affronts I've endured! Another Bonaparte! Shame!'

The coup d'État produces a veritable traumatism in him. Several months later, on March 5th, 1852, in a letter to his legal guardian Ancelle, he will produce this extraordinary expression:

'December 2nd has physically depoliticized me.'

We shall find the expected comment on the word 'physically' in a note for *Mon cœur mis à nu*:

'Two beautiful religions, immortal on walls, eternal obsessions of the People: a prick (the ancient phallus) and "Vive Barbès!" or "A bas Philippe!" or "Vive la République!"'

'Vive Barbès!', 'A bas Philippe!' specifically relate this passage to the revolution of 1848. The presence, in the same paragraph, of this other note is remarkable:

'Don't forget a portrait of Forgues, the pirate, the Plagiarist of letters.'

Émile Daurand-Forgues had published in 1846, in *Le Commerce*, an unauthorized version of *The Murders in the Rue Morgue* without mentioning Poe's name. This proximity underlines the relation of these two themes, fundamental in Baudelaire, indicating how the figure of Edgar Poe will succeed, in his private mythology, the figure of the crowd.

In his letter to his mother of March 27th, 1852, which he regards (having forgotten that of August 30th, 1851) as the first for nine months, he will say:

'As for political events and the overpowering influence they have had on me, I shall write to you about them another time.[1]

'Adieu, pity me when you think of the unbearable punishments I have prepared for myself.'[1]

To this letter he adds his two articles: 'Les Drames et les Romans honnêtes', 'L'École païenne', but he declares them already quite out of date:

'I won't be annoyed if you read them, when you have time. I doubt whether you'll understand them through and through; I'm not being impertinent, but they're *particularly Parisian*, and I doubt whether they can be understood outside the *milieux* for which and about which they were written.'

Let us note that he lumps together both 'Crépuscules', two poems of the crowd which were obviously to be part of *Les Limbes*, and which are admirable examples of the kind of poetry advocated in the article on Pierre Dupont.

(g) Napoléon III as executioner

Let us continue reading this note for *Mon cœur mis à nu* to the end:

'My intoxication in 1848 ...

'My rage over the coup d'État. How many affronts I've endured! Another Bonaparte! Shame!

'And yet everything has quieted down. Has the president no right he can invoke?

'What the Emperor Napoléon III is. What he's worth. Find the explanation of his nature, and of his providential mission.'

Some critics have been amazed by this conclusion,

---

[1] In the French there are two grammatical errors in these lines. Baudelaire, who attaches so much importance to propriety of diction, must have been disturbed as he wrote them.
—*Tr. note.*

which we must compare with a passage from a letter to Poulet-Malassis of March 20th, 1852 :

'No one agrees to take the *providential* point of view.

'You can guess what I mean. The president has given a kind of caress to men of letters … ',

because they have supposed that his notion of a providential mission implied on his part a certain esteem for Napoléon III and for his political system. Obviously nothing of the kind occurred. Another note for *Mon cœur mis à nu* makes this clear :

'All in all, in the eyes of history and of the French people, the great glory of Napoléon III will have been to prove that the first-comer can govern a great nation by controlling the telegraph and the press.

'Those who suppose that such things can be accomplished without the people's permission are fools – as are those who suppose that glory can only be based on virtue.

'Dictators are the servants of the people, nothing more – a miserable role, moreover – and glory is the result of the mind's adaptation to national stupidity.'

The providence in question is obviously that diabolic providence referred to at the beginning of the first study on Edgar Poe, on which Baudelaire was working at the very moment of the coup d'État, 'which offers disaster from the start'. Napoléon III is providential only as an executioner.

We recall that it is this kind of providential mission which Joseph de Maistre assigned to Napoléon I.

He is the bourgeois Attila. But Baudelaire cannot bring himself to consider the god of whom he is the scourge as just. 'Le Reniement de Saint Pierre', a poem which will play a prominent role in the history of his relations with his mother even after his death, since

Madame Aupick will try to remove it from her son's
Œuvres complètes, and since Asselineau will have to
threaten to abandon publication altogether, saying
'Charles is no longer here to protect himself', before
she yields to him, will appear in October 1852, in the
Revue de Paris:

> – Ah! Jésus, souviens-toi du Jardin des Olives!
> Dans ta simplicité tu priais à genoux
> Celui qui dans son ciel riait au bruit des clous
> Que d'ignobles bourreaux plantaient dans tes chairs
>   vives,
>
> Lorsque tu vis cracher sur ta divinité
> La crapule du corps de garde et des cuisines,
> Et lorsque tu sentis s'enfoncer les épines
> Dans ton crâne où vivait l'immense Humanité;
>   …
>
> Rêvais-tu de ces jours si brillants et si beaux
> Où tu vins pour remplir l'éternelle promesse,
> Où tu foulais, monté sur une douce ânesse,
> Des chemins tout jonchés de fleurs et de rameaux,
>
> Où le cœur tout gonflé d'espoir et de vaillance,
> Tu fouettais tous ces vils marchands à tour de bras,
> Où tu fus maître enfin? Le remords n'a-t-il pas
> Pénétré dans ton flanc plus avant que la lance?
>
> – Certes, je sortirai, quant à moi, satisfait
> D'un monde où l'action n'est pas la sœur de rêve;
> Puissé-je user du glaive et périr par le glaive!
> Saint Pierre a renié Jésus … il a bien fait!

It is Baudelaire himself, origin of the harm, who is
punished in Jeanne's disease; what in him is the mark
of his poetic vocation becomes an unjust punishment
when he communicates it to someone else. Similarly,

if he communicates to the politically impotent crowd his violent hatred for the bourgeoisie, common to all the romantics and a still more decisive mark of his vocation, then that crowd will itself become an anarchy, an atrocity, will end in misery and humiliation. Napoléon III as an executioner is only one of the symptoms of this disease.

(h) The death penalty

This is why, if the crowd, like Jeanne, can no longer serve him as an undistorting mirror, if the crowd, like Jeanne, will henceforth reflect an image of his own future so hideous that his sufferings will react in explosions of hatred, Baudelaire will maintain towards the crowd, as towards Jeanne, an attitude of extreme responsibility.

He will henceforth try to assume altogether the unjust punishment he has helped to inflict upon it, even in the smallest measure. To Napoléon III, the blind executioner who punishes innocent heads when the slightest crime is imputed to them, he will propose his own, *he* will be the voluntary criminal condemned to death; he will expect, he will seek out the condemnation he cannot naturally provoke save by a scandalously noble behaviour. Sacrifice will succeed direct political action.

Despite all his efforts to avoid such evidence, Baudelaire found the crowd indubitably right in 1848, and he was indubitably right to set himself to learn from it, but then a horrible misunderstanding occurs; he decides that he has mysteriously contaminated this crowd, and that it can recover its health only to the degree that he will have drawn the condemnation on his own head.

He must proceed in this way to achieve his human glory. Having surrendered himself to justice, he must expose the executioner's injustice. It is the entire society condemning him which would then be condemned.

Joseph de Maistre had regarded the French Revolution as an enormous sacrifice. Baudelaire takes up this idea in two notes for *Mon cœur mis à nu* :

'The Revolution and the cult of Reason prove the notion of sacrifice',

and :

'The Revolution, by sacrifice, confirms superstition.'

But of course Joseph de Maistre had never gone so far as to draw Baudelaire's conclusion : that to avoid sacrificing the crowd, it was necessary to sacrifice oneself, and if de Maistre has justified the death penalty by declaring that it was the condemned man himself who insisted upon it, he had not drawn the corollary that the death penalty was therefore truly justified only when the guilty man actually demanded it, and that it was therefore necessary to seek condemnation.

Here is how Baudelaire puts it in a note for *Mon cœur mis à nu* :

'The death penalty is the result of a mystical idea, totally misunderstood today. Its purpose is not to *save* society materially. Its goal is to *save* society and the guilty man spiritually. For the sacrifice to be perfect, there must be consent and joy on the victim's part. To chloroform a man condemned to death would be an impiety, for that would be robbing him of consciousness of his greatness as victim, and suppressing his chances of achieving Paradise.'

In an isolated note, certainly written before July 1856, since he announces on July 22nd to his mother :

'I've forgotten to tell you I'm going back to *La*

Revue des Deux Mondes with something very out of the way : – either a novel on *the ideal of conjugal love* – or a novel to justify and explain the sanctity of the death penalty',

we can read :

'Dandies.

'The opposite of Claude Gueux. Theory of sacrifice. Justification of the death penalty. The sacrifice is complete only by the victim's *sponte sua*.

'A man condemned to death who, having escaped the executioner and been freed by the people, would return to the executioner. New justification of the death penalty.'

Dandyism, the modern form of stoicism, is ultimately a religion whose only sacrament is suicide. For the poet, who is in reality what the dandy is only in appearance, this supreme moment becomes coextensive with his entire life; it is by his work and the condemnation that his work incurs that he will gradually put himself to death, and his trial will be the trial of all.

The dandy, in the sacramental moment of his suicide, is simultaneously victim and executioner, but he is both only in himself. In the poetry of danger, everything will be made general; the poet will alternately, and at length, be victim and executioner of the society which surrounds him.

In a note for *Mon cœur mis à nu* :

'The only great men are the poet, the priest and the soldier.

'The man who sings, the man who blesses, the man who sacrifices and is sacrificed.

'The rest are made for the whip.

'Let us beware of the people, of good sense, of the heart, of inspiration and of evidence.'

How much he had to beware of, indeed! How all this constantly returned to plague him!

We know that for Baudelaire the poet's function absorbs the priest's, since the poet is par excellence the man who can transmute his curse into a blessing; but his function could also absorb that of the soldier, the man who sacrifices himself, and even that of the man who sacrifices, as we learn from the note related to the *Argument du livre sur la Belgique* :

'When you talk about Revolution *in earnest*, you terrify them. *Old Maids*. When *I* consent to be a republican, *I do evil consciously*. Yes! *Vive la Révolution!*

'Still! After all!

'But I'm not anybody's dupe, I've never been a dupe! I say *Vive la Révolution!* the way I might say : *Vive la Destruction! Vive l'Expiation! Vive le Châtiment! Vive la mort!* Not only would I be happy to be a victim, but I wouldn't hate being an executioner – to experience the Revolution in both ways!'

The deplorable end of the Second Republic has disappointed him so deeply that he cannot risk a new wound as severe. And this is why he takes arms against his own heart, against his inspiration, his evidence, and even against his good sense. But if he is thus careful not to imagine a popular revolution that might succeed in abolishing the rule of money, this rule is still so damnable to him that even if the revolution must end in failure, it is preferable to the status quo.

In a fragment which must certainly be related to a draft for a prose-poem called 'Pile ou Face' :

'To have discovered a conspiracy. – That is almost a creative act. – The Empire is at my disposal. – Alternative, hesitation. – Why save the Empire? Why destroy it? *Hence*, heads or tails', we find a final comment on 'The Man of the Crowd', which shows us Baudelaire's continuing sensitivity to 'political agitation':

' – If the conspirators give ground, no further interest in my life. I am therefore interested in reawakening the conspiracy.

'(Portrait of the prince. Follies. These follies make him interesting for me. Old no-good: *inde* which vices and which qualities?)

'(Life is a game, the players number about three thousand million. The opportunities. The *moment* when loser takes all.) ...

'Yet no sooner is the conspiracy found than the young come back. Their eyes take an interest in life. Memories are no longer overwhelming. (A supper with the poor. There is, then, some virtue in humanity. Humility, usefulness.) – No sooner is the conspiracy eclipsed than the longing for nothingness returns.'

In case of an uprising, consequently, one can be sure that he would have been fascinated by the victor in the mêlée, and that he would have joined the rebels, not to help them achieve a victory which he longs for too grievously to be able to acknowledge this hope to himself, but to submit himself to the death penalty and help in the punishment at least of that bourgeoisie to which 'nature' will grant all too apparently an ignoble victory.

8

THE INTERCESSOR

(a) An admirable mother

Political events will naturally affect his inner life. If the mirror of the crowd no longer reflects anything but a horrible image of his future self, this in no way allows him to turn back towards the mirror that was Jeanne; it merely aggravates the former's horror. Hence, in the letter of March 27th, 1852, in which he tells his mother about the 'crushing' effects the recent political events have had on him, he declares:

'Jeanne has become an obstacle not only to my happiness – that would be a small thing, for I too can sacrifice my pleasures, and I have proved it – but to the perfecting of my mind. The nine months that have just gone by are a decisive test ... To unite all my thoughts in one, to give you a notion of all my reflections, I think *for good and all* that only the woman who has suffered and produced a child is man's equal. To give birth is the only thing that endows a woman with moral intelligence.'

One might suppose, reading these last lines thus detached from their context, that they were a homage to Madame Aupick, but other passages of this letter show that Baudelaire still has only a very meagre respect for the latter's 'moral intelligence'.

In the only original text that he will publish under his own name between this letter and May 1855, that is, until the end of the serial publication in *Le Pays* of the *Histoires* and *Nouvelles Histoires extraordinaires*, the splendid 'Morale du Joujou', he will accuse his mother publicly for the first time. He relates that she had taken him as a child to a lady named Panckoucke, who had asked him to pick out a toy from among a great number as a souvenir:

'I immediately seized the finest, the most expensive, the brightest, the newest, the strangest of the toys. My mother censured my indiscretion and stubbornly opposed my taking the toy away with me. She wanted me to be satisfied with an infinitely ordinary object. But I couldn't agree to it ...'

The sterility of the marriage with General Aupick was for him a further proof of its iniquity.

This ideal woman is obviously that other mother whom he wishes her to take as a model (as he himself henceforth takes for a model the son she had adopted), the woman referred to in the article he begs her to obtain, the major study on Edgar Poe, his life and works, which has just been published; it is to Maria Clemm that he then addresses this prayer:

'Admirable creature, as what is free dominates what is fatal, as the mind is above matter, so your affection soars above all human affections! May our tears cross the Ocean, the tears of all those who, like your poor Eddie, are miserable, anguished, and whom poverty and grief have often dragged into debauchery, may they reach your heart! May these lines, stamped with the sincerest and most respectful admiration, please your maternal eyes! Your quasi-divine image will constantly hover over the martyrology of literature!'

(b) Recognition

Jeanne the initiatrix is corrupted, the initiating crowd is corrupted in its turn. Will General Aupick have been right?

At this moment Baudelaire is saved by his discovery of a third intercessor, more precisely by the discovery that he can employ Edgar Poe as an intercessor, as a mirror of what he will be.

In a letter of 1864 the Thoré-Burger, the discoverer of Vermeer of Delft who stupidly reproached Manet for borrowing certain methods from Velasquez, he will reply:

'Well, then! I am accused of imitating Edgar Poe! Do you know why I have so patiently translated Poe? *Because he resembled me.* The first time I opened one of his books, I saw, with terror and delight, not only subjects I had dreamed of, but *sentences* I had conceived, which were written by him twenty years before. *Et nunc erudimini, vos qui judicatis! ...* '

Baudelaire is contracting the years, after the fact. In the fragment of his letter to Armand Fraisse, probably dating from 1858, he still knew that his 'recognition' had not been immediate:

'I can tell you something more singular and almost incredible. In 1846 or 1847, I came across several things by Edgar Poe: I experienced a peculiar commotion. His complete works having been collected only after his death in a single edition, I had the patience to make contact with some Americans living in Paris in order to borrow back numbers of magazines that had been edited by Edgar Poe. And then I found, believe it or not, poems and tales which I myself had vaguely thought of writing, and which Poe had been able to work out to perfection.'

In the dedication to Maria Clemm, published at the head of the first instalment of the *Histoires extra-ordinaires* in *Le Pays* for July 25th, 1854, he distinguished two periods in his knowledge of the American writer:

'Two years before the catastrophe which so horribly crushed this full and ardent existence, I was already making every effort to bring Edgar Poe to the attention of the literary men of my country. But then the permanent tempest of his life was unknown to me; I was unaware that these dazzling blooms were the product of volcanic soil, and when today I compare the false notion that I had of his life with what it really was – the Edgar Poe whom my imagination had created – rich, happy – a young gentleman of genius occasionally turning to literature among the thousand occupations of an elegant life – with the real Edgar – the pathetic Eddie, the one you have loved and sustained, the one I will introduce to France – this ironic antithesis fills me with a sympathy I can in no way check.'

Yet it is on October 15th, 1851, in a note whose addressee is unfortunately unknown, that he asks the receiver to obtain for him the 'Works of Edgar Poe, *and in particular the edition with the obituary notice in it, if there is one.*'

There was one, as a matter of fact, in the form of a venomous attack written by Rufus Griswold, the only biographical document Baudelaire possessed when he wrote his first study, already completed in February 1852.

In his letter to his mother of the following March 27th, in which he eagerly asks her to get a copy of this study, he speaks of Poe as a recent discovery:

'I have found an American author who has aroused

an incredible sympathy in me, and I have written two articles on his life and his works.'

After a year's silence, on March 26th, 1853, after listing for her the miseries of the last months, he calls her to witness:

'Do you now understand why, amid the hideous solitude that surrounds me, I have understood so well the genius of Edgar Poe, and why I have written his abominable life so well?'

(c) *The hatred of mercantile republics*

It is therefore at the very moment when the face of the crowd begins to waste away that Baudelaire recognizes himself in Edgar Poe. It is at the very moment when his democratic hopes are collapsing that he realizes that, in the very American republic which he would have eagerly proposed as a model to France a few months before, this Edgar Poe whom he so greatly admires was pursued by the same incomprehension as he himself was under the reign of Louis-Philippe. The sudden discovery of Poe's misery causes America's countenance to sicken as brutally as that of the French crowd. The violence of Baudelaire's hatred will again be the measure of his disappointment.

He apologizes thus in his dedication to Maria Clemm:

'By you, Madame, everything will be received with respect and gratitude, even the slight blame that may be aroused by the severity with which I have treated your compatriots, doubtless to comfort somewhat the hatred inspired in my free soul by the mercantile Republics and the physiocratic Societies', a severity which will increase to the point of absurdity in the 'Notes nouvelles sur Edgar Poe':

'To burn chained Negroes guilty of having felt their black cheeks flooded with the red of honour, to fire a revolver into the *parterre* of a theatre, to establish polygamy in the Western paradises which the Savages (this term seems unjust in itself) had not yet sullied with such shameful utopias, to advertise on walls, no doubt to consecrate the principle of limitless freedom, the *cure of nine-month diseases,* these are some of the salient features, some of the moral illustrations of the noble nation of Franklin, inventor of the shop-counter morality, the hero of an age dedicated to material things. It is good to keep the public aware of these wondrous brutalities, in a time when Americanomania has become almost a fashionable passion, when an archbishop can promise us with a straight face that Providence will soon call us to enjoy this transatlantic ideal.'

(*d*) 'Mesmeric Revelation'

Before reading the note by Rufus Griswold, before the collapse of the Second Republic, Baudelaire thought of Poe as the happy citizen of a nation where the most singular poet could be free, and if a few months after the explosion of 1848 he published in *La Liberté de penser* his first translation (after the unavowed version of the Reverend George Croly's 'Young Enchanter' ('Jeune Enchanteur') in *L'Esprit public* in 1846), of 'Mesmeric Revelation' ('Révélation magnétique'), a a surprising choice, if we fail to consider the circumstances, since this text is far from being one of Poe's finest, it is because he believed that henceforth the sun would rise in the west because he took the word 'revelation' in the title seriously.

In an admirable introductory note where he elaborates a fascinating theory of the novel which he will unfortunately abandon later, precisely because he will adopt, lazily one might say, Poe's condemnation of the long poem, and his eulogy of the brief tale, we can see to what degree he takes him at his word:

'Unity of organism, unity of fluid, unity of elemental substance, these recent theories have occasionally appeared by a singular accident, in the minds of poets, at the same time as in those of scholars and scientists.'

A few lines later, he insists:

'It is certain that these literary minds make singular journeys through philosophy. They take surprising turns and have sudden vistas along roads that are only their own.'

Four years later, in the 1852 study, 'Mesmeric Revelation' is still considered as a basic text:

'The author's point of departure has obviously been this: could one not, with the help of the unknown forces called mesmeric fluid, discover the law that governs remote worlds? The beginning is full of grandeur and solemnity. The doctor has mesmerized his patient merely to relieve him. "How do you think your present illness will result?" "I must die." "Does the idea of death afflict you?" "No – no!" The patient complains he is not being questioned properly. "What then shall I ask?" the doctor replies. "You must begin at the beginning." "The beginning! But where is the beginning?" (In a very low voice.) "You know that the beginning is GOD." "Is not God spirit?" "No." "Is God, then, material?" "No." There follows a tremendous theory of matter, of matter's gradations and the hierarchy of beings. I published this piece in one of the numbers of *La Liberté de penser* in 1848.'

But it is clear that this revelation is then subordinated to others which seem much more precious to

Baudelaire, and in the 'Notes nouvelles sur Edgar Poe', published as a preface to the *Nouvelles Histoires extraordinaires* in 1857, he reaches the point of giving 'Mesmeric Revelation' as the perfect example of those farces by which Poe created a magnificent parody of his time and his nation :

' ... always great, not only in his noble conceptions, but even as a joker.

II

'For he never was a dupe! – I don't believe that the Virginian who calmly wrote, in the middle of the democratic inundation : "the people have nothing to do with the laws save to obey them" had ever been a victim of our modern wisdom – and : "the nose of a people is its imagination; it is by the nose that it can always and easily be led" – and a hundred other passages in which the mockery rains down, thick as grapeshot, yet nonchalant and supercilious. The Swedenborgians congratulate him on his "Mesmeric Revelation", like those naive illuminati who once perceived in the author of *Le Diable amoureux* a Judas of their mysteries; they thank him for the great truths he has just proclaimed – for they have discovered (O verifiers of what cannot be verified!) that everything he has expressed is absolutely true – although at first, these good people admit, they had suspected that this might have been a mere fiction. Poe answers that, on his side, he has never suspected such a thing.'

(e) *The translation*

To be a dupe means, above all : to take one's desires for realities, in particular to believe that the people can effectively abolish the rule of the bourgeoisie.

In the late note related to the *Argument du livre sur la Belgique*, Baudelaire will return to the matter on his own account:

'Yes! *Vive la Révolution!*

'Still! All the same!

'But I am not a dupe, I have never been a dupe!'

And the dupery of democratic faith is directly related to the literal interpretation of a text like 'Mesmeric Revelation'. What Baudelaire discovered in the tale in 1848 was a philosophy related to that of certain socialist theoreticians, especially Fourier.

If he recognizes himself to this extent in the Virginian, at the moment when the coup d'État converts him to the ideas of Joseph de Maistre, it is because he has the impression of having made the same mistake about Poe that he has made about himself. He could believe that Poe was a democrat in 1848 exactly in the same way that he could believe himself to be a democrat; both reveal the same fascination with the crowd as spectacle, a characteristic of the poetic vocation, so that it is easy to understand Baudelaire's astonishment, once he has been disintoxicated, at discovering in Poe the corresponding expression of *his* disappointment.

Since Poe could reveal this fascination despite all his declarations, it is only natural that Baudelaire too should have revealed it. The contradiction is therefore not so great; the reversal is not betrayal. Poe's work contains the key to his own continuity.

It is because the two successive attitudes in Baudelaire correspond to two different readings of the same texts, or of texts written at the same time, by Poe, that he can subsequently assert, against all the evidence of his own discrepancies, that he has never been of another opinion.

Hence, Poe's example now saves him from silence and even from the destruction of the poetic work already written. The poems which should have gone into *Les Limbes* or *Les Lesbiennes* will consequently keep their value, whatever the contradictions with which his thought may contend, even as a joke. Poe's exemplary figure is the stratagem by which the poetic evidence, Baudelaire's poetic function, manages to survive despite this political confusion.

He knows that he is contradicting himself, but he also knows that through this contradiction something permanent is being affirmed. In order to continue to affirm this evidence despite that of December 2nd, which would appear to condemn it absolutely, Baudelaire must win the right to contradict himself. It is this right which Poe's image accords him, for in that image it seems to him that precisely these contradictions are resolved: he by absolute confidence in him: he, Poe, must know the secret. Physically depoliticized by December 2nd, Poe's example alone will permit him to recover his virility and his voice.

But seek this secret – the key and the formula – as he will, Baudelaire cannot localize it in any one phrase. It is there, of course, imprisoned in Poe's work, but in the work as a whole, no passage summarizes it in this regard; and it is to the imitation of the work as a whole that he must henceforth dedicate himself, as one speaks of the imitation of Christ, in order to win the right and the strength to publish *Les Fleurs du Mal*.

After this ascesis of several years' duration, he can finally present himself at the bar of judgment, present himself whole: his past – the poems and articles he has already written before December 1851 – as well as his future – those he will have written thereafter.

The anti-marriage of his liaison with Jeanne – black, carnal – of woman to woman – will be balanced and completed by this other anti-marriage – white, spiritual – of man to man, which is the translation of Edgar Poe.

(f) *An admirable son*

Three elements contribute to make the American poet into an ideal image of himself.

First of all, he has been able to win for himself the most admirable of mothers, a mother whom he owes not to Nature but whom his own greatness has deserved :

'Of course, the man who could have inspired so great a friendship had virtues, and his spiritual being must have been a powerfully attractive one.'

In describing Poe's connection with Maria Clemm, Baudelaire uses this remarkable expression which reveals in a particularly clear way the relationship between the figure of Poe and that of Jeanne :

'Edgar was both her son and her daughter.'

Secondly, he is dead, and consequently his entire production, which Baudelaire now studies in the first posthumous edition, can be regarded by him as contemporary; if there were reversals, developments in Poe, they are all already at the reader's disposal; the successive publication of individual works is henceforth opposed by the simultaneity of the *Œuvres complètes*.

Baudelaire will never question himself as to the variations Poe's thought might have undergone, and this is understandable, since, for him, one of the American's great virtues is to offer him simultaneously, in the same texts, what in himself is so painfully successive.

In every case, reversal is to be feared no longer; this work and this life are completed, definitive.

The catastrophe, with regard to Jeanne and the crowd, his first two mirrors, is that in his 'imitation' he corrupted them, communicated to them what in him was the distinctive sign of his vocation, and which in them became merely disease, curse without transfiguration, undeserved punishment.

As for Poe, not only is he himself a poet, but the fact that he is dead renders him absolutely invulnerable to any such contagion. He speaks to Baudelaire from a place where the latter's bad luck can no longer affect him. Imitation is henceforth possible in complete security. Poe's entire works become, in this regard, a 'mesmeric revelation'.

Lastly, this death itself is exemplary because it is 'almost a suicide'.

(g) Suicide and poetry

The existence of the dandy, that inferior version of the poet, culminates in the moment of his suicide, but he is then victim only of himself, his own executioner; his disappearance is without consequences. It is his own nothingness he is punishing. His death reveals him as pure appearance.

In poetic existence, which is the reality of which dandyism is only the shadow, there is indeed such a thing as a voluntary death, but this acquires quite different dimensions. The welcoming of death is no longer contained in the suspect brevity of a single, final conclusive moment, it is coextensive with the entire fulfilment of the work. It is the latter which is the long, incomparable weapon of the crime.

But above all, the poet is not only victim of himself, but of the entire people, the entire crowd; he is not only his own executioner but that of the entire crowd. His voluntary death, though perpetrated by the very *milieu* that has produced him, condemns the latter, and is of the gravest consequence to it.

Poe's work and life thus appear as one long suicide, in which he forces the society around him to perpetrate against him that crime which is transformed into a punishment.

'This death is almost a suicide – a suicide prepared long before. At least it caused the scandal of a suicide.'

In this scandal, society confers a sacred character upon its victim. As a matter of fact, whatever the faults it may have been able to blame the poet for, the death penalty which it has inflicted not by the intermediary of an executioner but directly, as though by its own hands, suddenly seems disproportionate. Society cannot say : justice has been done, order has been restored, we have saved ourselves an executioner; it is obliged to complain : things shouldn't have gone so far, and we must punish this dead man for having caused this disturbance, for having revealed this injustice; yet the dead man henceforth escapes any human punishment. Human justice remains with this wound.

'*Society* regards the man who commits suicide as insolent; it would gladly chastise certain funereal remains, like that wretched soldier, afflicted with vampirism, whom the sight of a corpse aroused to the point of madness.'

Astonishing comparison! The victim, henceforth invulnerable, acquires a prodigious power of seduction. The crowd, the bourgeois crowd that has persecuted him, suddenly feels a hideous desire for his corpse which will never leave it in peace; but it doesn't matter whether the crowd is the bourgeois crowd, or the crowd as a whole in so far as it lets itself be led by the bourgeoisie, for the American poet could naturally maintain with the other face of the crowd, the black and accursed crowd of the poor, a mysterious and characteristic understanding:

'It appears that Poe was very undemanding as to his audience. Whether his listeners were capable of understanding his tenuous abstractions, or of admiring the glorious conceptions that continually flashed across the dark sky of his mind, did not disturb him at all. He would sit in a tavern, beside some sordid wretch, and quite seriously explain the outlines of his terrible book *Eureka* with an implacable *sang-froid*, as if he were dictating it to a secretary or arguing with Kepler, Bacon or Swedenborg. Never did a man free himself more completely from the rules of society, concern himself less with those around him, never bothering to ask why, on certain days, they refused to let him into places where *respectable people* drink. Never has any society forgiven such things, still less an English or American society.'

(h) 'Berenice'

It is remarkable that the work by Poe that Baudelaire analyses at greatest length in the 1852 study is, in fact, a story of vampirism, 'Berenice', in which the wretched hero's 'trances' focus on his victim's mouth, on the instrument of her voice:

' ... Aegeus is to marry her cousin. In the time of her incomparable beauty, he never spoke a single word of love to her; but now he feels great friendship for her, and great pity. Moreover, does she not have the enormous attraction of a problem? And, as he confesses, *"in the strange anomaly of his existence, feelings had never been of the heart, and passions always were of the mind."* One evening, in the library, the narrator finds Berenice standing before him. Either by a trick of the mind or because of the uncertain twilight of the room, he sees her as taller than usual. He stares for a long time in silence at this slender phantom which, with the painful coquetry of a woman grown ugly, tries to give him a smile, a smile that means: "I have changed, haven't I?" And then she shows her teeth between her poor, twisted lips. "Would to God that I had never beheld them, or that, having done so, I had died!"'

Now the teeth have become an obsession in Aegeus' mind. For two days and a night, he sits nailed to the spot, with ghostly teeth floating around him. The teeth are daguerreotyped in his mind – long and narrow, like the teeth of a dead horse; not a speck, not a shade, not a notch has escaped him. He shudders in horror when he realizes that he has come to assign to them a capacity for feeling and a power of moral expression even when unassisted by the lips. 'Of Mademoiselle Salle it has been well said : *"que tous ses pas étaient des sentiments,"* and of Berenice I more seriously believed *que toutes ses dents étaient des idées.*'

'By the end of the second day, Berenice has died; Aegeus dares not refuse to go into the room where the body lies and say a last farewell to his cousin's remains. The heavy curtains of the bed which he raises fall over his shoulders and enclose him in the most intimate communion with the dead woman. Strangely, a strap fastened under her chin has come undone. The teeth gleam again, implacably white and long. He tears himself away from the bed and rushes away, horrified.

'Thereafter, darkness increases in his mind, and the tale becomes troubled and confused. He comes to himself sitting in the library, beside a table with a lamp and an open book on it, and he shudders as his eyes fall upon this sentence: *Dicebant mihi sodales si sepulchrum amicae visitarem, curas meas aliquantulum fore levatas.* Beside the book is an ebony box. Why was it there? Did it not belong to the family physician? A servant enters, pale and distressed; he speaks in a low, husky voice. However, from his broken phrases it is apparent that a grave has been violated, great screams have been heard, a corpse, still warm and palpitating, has been found at the edge of its grave, bleeding and disfigured. He points to Aegeus' own clothes: they are muddy and bloodstained. He takes his hand; it has been torn by human nails. He directs his attention to an object leaning against the wall: it is a spade. With a terrible shriek, Aegeus flings himself upon the box; but in his weakness and agitation it slips from his hand, and as it drops on the floor it releases some instruments of dental surgery that scatter with a dreadful clatter of iron, intermingled with the cursed objects of his hallucination. In his absence of consciousness, the wretch has torn his *idée fixe* from the jaws of his cousin, buried mistakenly during one of her epileptic fits.'

'Berenice' is the first tale Baudelaire translated after his 'conversion'. It is accompanied, in *L'Illustration* of April 17th, 1852, by a note certainly written largely by him, but of which he obviously could not have read the proofs, so that in certain passages we are reduced to conjecture; in part, it says:

'The responsibility for a share of his vices, notably his drunkenness, must be assigned to the severe society in which Providence has imprisoned him.'

(i) *Aegeus, Theseus and Hippolytus*

The name Berenice is obviously related to her hair:
'innumerable ringlets now of a vivid yellow, and
jarring discordantly, in their fantastic character, with
the reigning melancholy of the countenance' (we
know that the Egyptian queen of this name dedicated
a lock of her hair to Aphrodite, and that Callimachus
declared in a poem that he had seen it among the
constellations, a flattery that modern astronomers
have effected in reality); as for the name Aegeus, king
of Athens, whose second wife Medea tried to kill his
son Theseus, it obviously refers us to Edgar Poe's
adoptive father, Arthur Allan:

'Meanwhile Mr Allan, whose first wife has died,
married a lady many years younger than himself. He
was then sixty-five. It was said that Mr Poe behaved
improperly to the lady and that he mocked the marriage. The old gentleman wrote him a severe letter,
to which Poe replied even more bitterly. The rift
could not be bridged, and a short time after Mr
Allan died without leaving a penny to his adopted
son.

'At this point in the biographical notices, I find some
highly mysterious remarks, obscure and singular al-
lusions as to the behaviour of our future author. Quite
hypocritically, and professing that he will say absolutely nothing, that there are things that must always remain hidden (why?), that in certain outrageous
cases silence must take precedence over truth, the
biographer casts a serious aspersion upon Mr Poe. The
damage is all the greater in that it remains veiled in
obscurity. What the devil can he mean? Is he in-
sinuating that Poe tried to seduce his adoptive father's
wife? It is really impossible to tell. But I believe I

have put the reader sufficiently on guard against the American biographers ...'

Throughout this passage, we feel Arthur Allan's character shifting from Aegeus to old Theseus. Baudelaire interprets the quarrel between Poe and his adoptive father on the model of Racine's *Phèdre*. In Poe he discerns a new Hippolyte.

(j) 'Une Martyre'

The importance which 'Berenice' had for Baudelaire sheds a new light on a certain number of the poems in *Les Fleurs du Mal*, particularly 'Une Martyre', a drawing by an unknown master;

> L'homme vindicatif que tu n'as pu vivante,
> 　　Malgré tant d'amour assouvir,
> Combla-t-il sur ta chair inerte et complaisante
> 　　L'immensité de son désir?
>
> Réponds, cadavre impur! et par tes tresses roides
> 　　Te soulevant d'un bras fiévreux,
> Dis-moi, tête effrayante, a-t-il sur tes dents froides
> 　　Collé les suprêmes adieux?

If Baudelaire's poems and notes so often describe physical love by means of comparisons borrowed from the vocabulary of torture, it is because the victim assumes, for the man who inflicts death, an absolutely exceptional erotic attraction. The martyr (of whichever sex) acquires an immutable physical beauty which will torment the executioner:

> Loin du monde railleur, loin de la foule impure,
> 　　Loin des magistrats curieux,
> Dors en paix, dors en paix, étrange créature,
> 　　Dans ton tombeau mystérieux;

Ton époux court le monde, et ta forme immortelle
    Veille près de lui quand il dort;
Autant que toi sans doute il te sera fidèle,
    Et constant jusques à la mort.

9

LE VIN

(a) *Systematic alcoholism*

It is by wine that Poe will gradually commit suicide or, more exactly, it is by wine that the mocking world, the corrupt crowd will execute him, in so far as wine will be for him the only means of continuing his literature despite this crowd.

For it is not the pleasures of oblivion that Poe sought in the bottle, but, on the contrary, the means of regaining possession of a memory he was being urged to lose. The best example Baudelaire can find of this fidelity by wine is the hideous drunkenness by which the American poet caused his second marriage to collapse :

'Thus resorting to his vice in order to rid himself of an affront to the poor dead woman whose image still survived within him and whom he had splendidly celebrated in *Annabel Lee*.'

According to Baudelaire, Poe's drunkenness was deadly only because it was systematic, because it was a literary method.

In this regard, our poet's thought has made a leap between the 1852 study and that of 1856 which opens the volume of *Histoires extraordinaires* published on March 12th. In the first study, as a matter of fact, the pleasure of oblivion is offered as the basic reason for Poe's drunkenness, and Baudelaire is content to note, as an anomaly of first importance, though one for

which he is as yet unable to account, the relation between this drunkenness and creation :

'It is an astonishing fact, but one attested by all who
knew him, that neither the purity, the polish, nor the
clarity of his thought, nor his diligence in his work
and in his difficult research, were altered by his terrible habit. The creation of most of his fine things
either preceded or followed one of these bouts. After
the publication of "Eureka", he abandoned himself to
drink with a frenzy. In New York, the very morning
"The Raven" was published, when Poe's name was in
every mouth and everyone was buying his poem, he
was staggering down Broadway, bumping into the
buildings.'

In 1856, the traumatism of the coup d'État having
faded, Baudelaire is capable of linking these facts to
the series of ideas he had developed just before the
crisis, in the essay published in March 1851 in *Le
Messager de l'Assemblée* : 'Du Vin et du Haschisch
comparés comme moyens de multiplication de l'individualité' :

'It is incontestable that – like those fugitive and
fabulous impressions, all the more fabulous the more
fugitive they are, which sometimes follow an external
symptom, a kind of warning like a sound of a bell, a
musical note or a forgotten perfume, and which are
themselves followed by an event similar to an already
known event that occupied the same place in a previously revealed series – like those singular periodic
dreams that haunt our sleep – there exists in drunkenness not only the enchantment of dreams, but trains
of reasoning which require, to reproduce themselves,
the circumstances which have generated them in the
first place. If the reader has followed me without re-
pugnance, he has already divined my conclusion : I

believe that in many cases, though certainly not in all, Poe's drunkenness was a mnemonic means, a method of work, a deadly method, but one appropriate to his impassioned nature. The poet had learned to drink the way a scrupulous literary man trains himself by keeping notebooks. He could not resist the desire to recover the marvellous or dreadful visions, the subtle conceptions which he had encountered in a preceding tempest; they were old acquaintances who imperatively attracted him, and to meet them again he took the most dangerous, but the most direct, path. A part of what today comprises our pleasure is what has killed him.'

(b) 'Le Vin des chiffonniers'

Baudelaire distinguishes two periods in Poe's drunkenness : it is first a hostile society which obliges him, by injustice and incomprehension, to seek an outlet in this vice, as it obliges the people to do the same thing.

In the 1851 essay, 'Du Vin et du Haschisch comparés comme moyens de multiplication de l'individualité', previous to the crisis, he indicated the close relationship between wine and what is darkest in the crowd, discovering in drunkenness an image, a prefiguration of the collapse of the hierarchy, the future revolution of which that of 1848 could only be the prelude :

'Let us descend a little lower. Consider one of these mysterious creatures living, so to speak, on the excrement of a great city; for there are singular professions, their number is enormous. I have sometimes thought with terror that there were professions which involved no joy, professions without pleasure, exhaustions without relief, pains without compensation – I was wrong. Here is a man whose job is to sweep up the day's rubbish in the capital. Everything the great city has rejected, everything it has lost, disdained, broken, he catalogues, he collects ... He arrives bobbing his head and stumbling along the cobbles, like young poets who spend their days wandering through the streets in search of rhymes. He talks to himself; he pours out his soul in the cold night air. His words are a magnificent monologue that puts the most lyrical tragedies to shame. "Forward march! Division, head, army!" Exactly like Bonaparte's death agonies on Saint Helena! Apparently the number seven has been changed into an iron sceptre, and his straw cloak into an imperial mantle. Now he compliments his army. The battle is won, but the day has been hot. He rides under triumphal arches. His heart is happy. He listens delightedly to the cheers of an enthusiastic crowd. Soon he will dictate a code of laws superior to all those known to mankind. He solemnly swears he will make his people happy. Poverty and vice have vanished from mankind!

'And yet his back and loins are crushed by the weight of his burden. He is tormented by household cares, battered by forty years of work. Age is creeping up on him. But wine, like a new Pactolus, floods an intellectual gold through a languishing humanity. Like good kings, wine rules by its services and sings its exploits through the throats of its subjects.

'On earth's globe, there is a numberless, nameless crowd whose sleep cannot anaesthetize its sufferings. Wine composes songs and poems for them.'

This passage is an amplification of the poem 'Le Vin des chiffonniers', already composed but still unpublished, which Baudelaire will include in *Les Fleurs du Mal* :

Souvent à la clarté rouge d'un réverbère
Dont le vent bat la flamme et tourmente le verre,
Au cœur d'un vieux faubourg, labyrinthe fangeux
Où l'humanité grouille en ferments orageux,

On voit un chiffonnier qui vient, hochant la tête,
Butant, et se cognant aux murs comme un poète,
Et, sans prendre souci des mouchards, ses sujets,
Épanche tout son cœur en glorieux projets …

An examination of the variants shows that the
many corrections made in proof were mostly intended
to make the text conform more closely to his 1851
exegesis. Thus in the earliest manuscript, probably
previous to 1848, the poem ends with these lines:

C'est ainsi que la vin règne par ses bienfaits
Et chante ses exploits par le gosier de l'homme
Grandeur de la bonté de Celui que tout nomme,
Qui nous avait déjà donné le doux sommeil,
Et voulut ajouter le Vin, fils du Soleil,
Pour réchauffer le cœur et calmer la souffrance
De tous les malheureux qui souffrent en silence.

In the manuscript of the 'Douze poèmes' which
dates from 1851, in other words contemporaneous for
the most part with the essay 'Du Vin et du Haschisch',
these seven lines have become the two following
strophes:

C'est ainsi qu'à travers l'humanité frivole
Le vin roule de l'or comme un nouveau Pactole
Par le gosier de l'homme il chante ses exploits
Et pars ses bienfaits règne ainsi que les bons Rois.

Pour apaiser le cœur et calmer le souffrance
De tous les innocents qui meurent en silence,

Dieu leur avait déjà donné le doux sommeil;
Il ajouta le vin, fils sacré du Soleil.

If we compare this version with that of the first
edition of *Les Fleurs du Mal*, we shall be surprised by
the progress made in impiety, in revolutionary ardour,
whereas in principle Baudelaire had renounced his
democratic ideas years before; in a word, by the closer
conformity of the text to the ideas expressed in the
essay. We see how reluctant Baudelaire's conversion
is, and how strongly, under the mask borrowed from
Joseph de Maistre, all his ideas, all his old sentiments
subsist, though he no longer dares confess them, even
to himself, save in verse, out of disappointment, and
out of fear of being duped.

It is at this point, in fact, that he adds the third
strophe :

Il prête des serments, dicte des lois sublimes,
Terrasse les méchants, relève les victimes,
Et sous le firmament comme un dais suspendu
S'enivre des splendeurs de sa propre vertu.

In the final strophes, *Humanité* and *Vin* assume
capital letters, which the word *rois* loses. The innocent become old derelicts. God has given them only
sleep, and even then because he has been seized by
remorse, and it is *l'Homme*, with a capital H, who has
countered with wine; which gives us :

C'est ainsi qu'à travers l'Humanité frivole
Le vin roule de l'or, éblouissant Pactole;
Par le gosier de l'homme il chante ses exploits
Et règne par ses dons ainsi que les vrais rois.

Pour noyer la rancœur et bercer l'indolence
De tous ces vieux maudits qui meurent en silence,

Dieu, saisi de remords, avait fait le sommeil;
L'Homme ajouta le Vin, fils sacré du Soleil!

In a final correction, that of the second edition of
1861, God will no longer even be *saisi* but merely
touché by remorse.

Baudelaire has never wavered in his defence of the
people's drunkenness, the only outlet society grants
its most disinherited victims. It is a crime, of course,
to leave only this outlet, but a still greater crime to
try to forbid even this one. When wine is denied to
the people, it is because the ruling class can no longer
endure the accusation that it reads in their drunkenness; it attempts to silence this voice.

In the essay 'Morale du Joujou', the only original
text Baudelaire published under his own name between the 1852 study of Edgar Poe and the end of the
serial publication of *Histoires extraordinaires* (and of
Nouvelles Histoires) in *Le Pays*, he mentions parents
who never give their children toys:

'These are the same people who gladly give a franc
to a poor man, on condition that he chokes himself
with bread, and always refuse him two sous for a
glass of wine. When I think of a certain class of ultra-
rational and anti-poetic persons through whom I have
suffered so greatly, I always feel hatred tightening
and harrowing my nerves.'

In *Les Paradis artificiels*, if the theme of wine is
developed no further, it none the less expressly links
his study to 'Le Vin des chiffonniers':

'It is this corruption of the sense of infinity that, to
my view, causes all culpable excess, from the solitary
and concentrated intoxication of the literary man
who, obliged to seek in opium relief from physical
pain, and having thus discovered a source of morbid

pleasure, gradually makes it his sole medicine and ultimately the sun of his spiritual life, to the drunkenness of the most loathsome derelict who, his brain inflamed with glory, sprawls absurdly in the garbage of the street.'

The literary man in question is obviously Thomas de Quincey, but in the expression 'solitary and concentrated intoxication' we also recognize the 'literary method' of Edgar Poe.

(c) The weapon of wine

Hence Poe's drunkenness is primarily 'popular', an outlet he is forced to resort to by American society, but as such it would not be deadly, on the contrary it would offer a means of survival.

Poe's genius will be to make an incomparable evil out of this affliction to which he is condemned, a deadly weapon out of this weapon with which he has been struck, thereby obliging this society to recognize, under the minor scandal of drunkenness, the major scandal of suicide.

It is because American society has reduced him to the point where he can no longer be a poet save with the help of alcohol that Poe has thrown himself on this deadly remedy, happy to regain, in spite of everything, this forbidden paradise, happy to disturb, by his spectacular death, the minds of his executioners :

'Thus vanished from this world one of the greatest heroes of literature, the man of genius who had written, in "The Black Cat", these prophetic words : *"What disease is like alcohol!"* '

Those who condemn a child to poetry are unaware what paradise his unhappiness will oblige him to discover; those who condemn a people to drunkenness have no idea what utopias, what prospects wine will suddenly suggest to them.

'He was, thus, an admirable protest; he was this protest, and he made it *in his own way*.'[1]

The protest consisted not only of the fact that he transformed his drunkenness into suicide (admirably, exemplarily making the discoveries of alcohol serve the discoveries of poems), but also of his way of drinking :

'I have discovered that he did not drink *en gourmand*, but *en barbare*, with an activity and an economy of time that were quite American, as though accomplishing a homicidal function, as though having *something* to kill within himself, *a worm that would not die*.'[2]

This 'aristocrat of nature' drinks like a rag-picker; he seeks no excuse in the refinement of taste, he never suggests that his palate takes any pleasure; he hasn't time. It is intoxication that he ostentatiously seeks, and intoxication alone, and in his very act of drinking he will be a caricature of those who condemn him and whom he condemns, for he will put the same activity and economy into the search for spiritual gold as they in their pursuit of material gold. Baudelaire then attributes to Poe the external aspect of the executioner, mirror of the unconscious executioners of his society; his scandalous death will suddenly show them what they were; he will be *his own executioner* in so far as in his good faith he makes himself their accomplice, tries to satisfy them, to put himself out of the way, to kill this worm that will not die, this demon of poetry to which they have so indiscreetly consigned him.

[1] 'in his own way' is in English in the text. – *Tr. note.*
[2] 'a worm that would not die' is in English in the text. – *Tr. note.*

(d) 'Le Vin de l'assassin'

The role that wine plays in the life and death of Edgar Poe entirely justifies the privileged place assigned to it in the first edition of *Les Fleurs du Mal*, between 'La Révolte' and 'La Mort'. For Baudelaire, poetry involves the danger of death, because it is a rebellion; Edgar Poe's alcoholism is an admirable expression of this connection.

The significance he attached to this situation is emphasized by the letter of Saturday, May 16th, 1857, to his publisher Poulet-Malassis:

'And the table of contents? You can begin it.

'Here is the end:

94.   Le Vin des chiffonniers.
95.   Le Vin de l'assassin.
96.   Le Vin du solitaire.
97.   Le Vin des amants.
     LA MORT
98.   La Mort des amants.
99.   La Mort des pauvres.
100. La Mort des artistes.'

'La Mort des amants' obviously continues 'Le Vin des amants', 'La Mort des artistes' corresponds to 'Le Vin du solitaire', 'La Mort des pauvres' to 'Le Vin des chiffonniers'.

If the section 'Le Vin' has changed place in the second edition of *Les Fleurs du Mal* (1861), where it is no longer between 'La Révolte' and 'La Mort', but between the 'Tableaux parisiens' and 'Les Fleurs du Mal' proper, this is first of all because the addition of three new poems in 'La Mort' destroyed the symmetry of the two sections, because Baudelaire wanted to link the theme of Wine more closely to that of the city's ferment, and above all because he had meanwhile published *Les Paradis artificiels*, in which he had opened a second trial of hashish (condemned too rapidly in 1851 in favour of wine), and because at this moment the most enlightening example of 'the solitary and concentrated intoxication of the literary man' will have become De Quincey's opium addiction, an even more striking but even more dangerous example of pure poetic intoxication.

As for 'Le Vin de l'assassin', it was already his death :

> – Me voilà libre et solitaire!
> Je serai ce soir ivre mort;
> Alors, sans peur et sans remord,
> Je me coucherai sur la terre,
>
> Et je dormirai comme un chien!
> Le chariot aux lourdes roues
> Chargé de pierres et de boues,
> Le wagon enragé peut bien
>
> Écraser ma tête coupable
> Ou me couper par le milieu,
> Je m'en moque comme de Dieu,
> Du Diable ou de la Sainte Table!

This poem was published in 1848 in *L'Écho des Marchands de vin*. We can imagine Baudelaire's surprise upon discovering in Poe's biography the proud answer to his question of that time :

> Nul ne peut me comprendre. Un seul
> Parmi ces ivrognes stupides
> Songea-t-il dans ses nuits morbides
> A faire du vin un linceul?

Meanwhile, moreover, the poet had singularly identified himself with the murderer of his poem, as is indicated in the letter to his mother of March 27th,

1852, which we have consulted so many times already, the first letter he has written her since the coup d'état, since his 'conversion', since his reading of Poe's biography and his decision to dedicate himself to the systematic imitation of the American poet. It is this letter which the critics generally use to degrade Jeanne's character, despite all Baudelaire's protests elsewhere, because in it he announces his decision to leave her for ever, a decision without consequences.

'I have tears of shame and fury in my eyes as I write you this; and to be honest I am glad there is no weapon here with me; I am thinking of the cases in which it is impossible for me to obey the dictates of reason, and of the terrible night I split open her head with the console table.'

We unfortunately do not possess any other information about that 'terrible night': it is apparent that Baudelaire has here become almost the murderer of his poem, but that once the wound was inflicted, the victim acquired such beauty that the executioner has become her slave more than ever. 'Le Vampire' corresponds to 'Le Vin de l'assassin':

> Toi qui, comme un coup de couteau,
> Dans mon cœur plaintif es entrée;
> Toi qui forte comme un troupeau
> De démons, vins folle et parée,
>
> De mon esprit humilié
> Faire ton lit et ton domaine;
> – Infâme à qui je suis lié
> Comme le forçat à la chaîne,
>
> Comme au jeu le joueur têtu,
> Comme à la bouteille l'ivrogne,

Comme aux vermines la charogne
Maudite, maudite sois-tu !

J'ai prié le glaive rapide
De conquérir ma liberté,
Et j'ai dit au poison perfide
De secourir ma lâcheté.

Hélas ! le poison et le glaive
M'ont pris en dédain et m'ont dit :
'Tu n'es pas digne qu'on t'enlève
A ton esclavage maudit

'Imbécile ! – de son empire
Si nos efforts te délivraient,
Tes baisers ressusciteraient
Le cadavre de ton vampire !'

The rhymes of this poem are generally alternate, save in two strophes where they follow an *abba* scheme, like those of 'Le Vin de l'assassin', in particular the strophe which refers to wine. A certain number of passages of the latter poem could be included without difficulty in 'Le Vampire', particularly the following two, difficult to explain in their present context and which are suddenly illuminated if one compares the two works :

Cette crapule invulnérable
Comme les machines de fer
Jamais, ni l'été ni l'hiver,
N'a connu l'amour véritable,

Avec ses noirs enchantements,
Son cortège infernal d'alarmes,
Ses fioles de poison, ses larmes,
Ses bruite de chaîne et d'ossements !

All of this in order to stress the relationship between the two poems. The theme of 'Le Vin de l'assassin' will haunt Baudelaire for years, and this in relation not only to his attack on Jeanne, but also to his 'imitation' of Poe. Indeed, a letter to the actor J. H. Tisserant (whom Baudelaire had met some days before and who had been impressed by a project for a play), dated January 28th, 1854, informs us that this project was none other than a reworking and development of the poem published six years before in *L'Écho des Marchands de vin*, to which he adds a *dénouement* taken almost word for word from what will be the first of the *Nouvelles Histoires extraordinaires*, 'Le Démon de la Perversité' (The Imp of the Perverse).

The poem opens with these lines:

> Ma femme est morte, je suis libre!
> Je puis donc boire tout mon soûl.
> Lorsque je rentrais sans un sou,
> Ses cris ne déchiraient la fibre.

Here is their translation into prose in the letter to Tisserant:

'The man reappears: *I am free! – Poor angel, how she must have suffered!*'

But then this expression '*I am free*' constitutes the transition to the end of Poe's tale, which takes up the fundamental Baudelairian theme of the voluntary death penalty:

' ... *I am safe.*

'One day, whilst sauntering along the streets, I arrested myself in the act of murmuring, half aloud, these customary syllables. In a fit of petulance, I remodelled them thus: "I am safe – I am safe – yes – if I be not fool enough to make open confession!"

'No sooner had I spoken these words, than I felt an

icy chill creep to my heart. I had had some experience
in these fits of perversity (whose nature I have been
at some trouble to explain), and I remembered well
that in no instance I had successfully resisted their
attacks. And now my own casual self-suggestion, that
I might possibly be fool enough to confess the murder
of which I had been guilty, confronted me, as if the
very ghost of him whom I had murdered – and
beckoned me on to death.

'At first, I made an effort to shake off this nightmare of the soul. I walked vigorously – faster – still
faster – at length I ran. I felt a maddening desire to
shriek aloud. Every succeeding wave of thought over-
whelmed me with new terror, for, alas! I well, too
well, understood that to *think*, in my situation, was to
be lost. I still quickened my pace. I bounded like a
madman through the crowded thoroughfares. At
length, the populace took the alarm and pursued me.
I felt *then* the consummation of my fate. Could I
have torn out my tongue, I would have done it – but
a rough voice resounded in my ears – a rougher grasp
seized me by the shoulder. I turned – I gasped for
breath. For a moment I experienced all the pangs of
suffocation; I became blind, and deaf, and giddy; and
then some invisible fiend, I thought, struck me with his
broad palm upon the back. The long-imprisoned secret
burst forth from my soul.

'They say that I spoke with a distinct enunciation,
but with marked emphasis and passionate hurry, as
if in dread of interruption before concluding the brief
but pregnant sentences that consigned me to the hangman and to hell.

'Having related all that was necessary for the fullest
judicial conviction, I fell prostrate in a swoon.

'But why shall I say more? Today I wear these chains, and am *here*! Tomorrow I shall be fetterless! – *but where?*'

We find this *dénouement* again, summarized and adapted, in the letter to Jules Tisserant:

'Here in a few words is the description of the *dénouement*. Our man has escaped. – We are now in a seaport. – He thinks of getting himself taken on as a sailor. – He drinks dreadfully; wineshops, sailors' taverns, *musicos*. – This idea: "*I am free, free, free!*" has become an *idée fixe*, an obsession. "I am *free*! – I am *calm*! – *No one will ever know*." – And as he goes on drinking, and has been drinking heavily for several months, his will shrinks further – and the *idée fixe* finally comes to light in a few words spoken aloud. As soon as he notices this, he tries to stun himself by *drink*, by *walking*, by *running* – but the strangeness of his manner causes him to be noticed. – A man running has obviously *done something*. He is stopped; then – with *a volubility, an eagerness, an extraordinary emphasis,* with extreme attention to detail – very quickly, very quickly, as if he feared not having time to finish, he tells his crime in all its details. – Then he falls in a dead faint.'

(e) 'L'Héautontimorouménos'

In the anecdote reported in the study on 'Edgar Poe, sa vie et ses œuvres' which introduces *Histoires extraordinaires*, the only previously unpublished material in this first volume of Baudelaire's, published on Wednesday, March 12th, 1856, the vampire is the soldier 'whom the sight of a corpse aroused to the point of frenzy'. It is the soldier again in the poem 'Une Martyre', it is Aegeus in 'Bernice'. The vampire is the executioner; but in the poem that bears this title, the vampire is Jeanne – is the victim.

In the famous 'Héautontimorouménos', certainly dedicated to Jeanne under the veil of the mysterious initials J.G.F. which we shall find again at the head of the dedication of *Les Paradis artificiels* (in a draft of the latter, we shall read the following sentence: 'I want this dedication to be unintelligible'; he means, of course, unintelligible except to the woman it is intended for),

in which he resumes the versification of 'Le Vin de l'assassin', a versification which we encounter elsewhere in the first edition of *Les Fleurs du Mal*, only in 'L'Irrémédiable', a conclusion to this whole group, in 'A celle qui est trop gaie', and in the group about 'Le Chat', though it should be noted that, in these last texts, we do not find the enjambments characteristic of 'Le Vin de l'assassin', 'Le Vampire' and 'L'Héautontimorouménos'),

a versification he will resume in 1860 in the 'Chanson d'après-midi':

> Et tu connais la caresse
> Qui fait revivre les morts!

Baudelaire presents himself to us not only as 'his own executioner', but as his own vampire. Joanne was his mirror, a mirror that has been corrupted, but he is also her mirror.

> Dans nos deux esprits, ces miroirs jumeaux,

'La Mort des amants' told us;

> Je suis le sinistre miroir
> Où le mégère se regarde!

said 'L'Héautontimorouménos' (we have already

noticed, in 'Sed non satiata', that the name Megaera designated Jeanne).

> Je suis la plaie et le couteau !
> Je suis le soufflet et la joue !
> Je suis les membres et la roue,
> Et la victime et le bourreau !
>
> Je suis de mon cœur le vampire,
> – Un de ces grands abandonnés
> Au rire éternel condamnés,
> Et qui ne peuvent plus sourire !

His own executioner, his own vampire, he implicates the entire society in his own torture; he shows the entire society as victim, awakens it as redresser, reveals it to itself as both martyr and vampire.

The last lines of 'L'Héautontimorouménos' naturally refers us to the Reverend Maturin's *Melmoth*, and if we turn to the essay 'De l'essence du rire', which Baudelaire had been thinking about for a long time but which will be published for the first time only in *Le Portefeuille* on July 8th, 1855, we shall see that he mentions Melmoth immediately after the passage we have already quoted apropos of stumbling, a passage that directly suggests the last part of our dream : 'It's not *me* that's falling; *I'm* walking properly; *my* footing is firm and assured.'

And in the next section of this essay, we learn that the laughter of the 'pale and bored Melmoth', 'the highest expression of pride' which 'perpetually accomplishes its function while tearing and scorching the lips of the unpardonable laugher', is not the act of a few isolated individuals, but that it must rack whole nations before it can be transcended by a 'limpid poetry profound as nature'.

'Comparing, as we are entitled to do, humanity with man, we see that, like Virginia, primitive tribes do not conceive of caricature and have no comedies (sacred books, whatever their provenance, never laugh), and that, gradually advancing towards the cloudy peaks of intelligence, or bending over the murky furnaces of metaphysics, the nations begin laughing diabolically with Melmoth's laugh.'

We mark the transition from Virginia, Bernardin de Saint-Pierre's heroine alluded to early in the essay, to Virginia, the native state of Edgar Poe.

10

HISTOIRES and NOUVELLES HISTOIRES

(a) The sequence of publication

If the book in our dream is the *Histoires extraordinaires*, it is none the less true that not everything in this volume is present in the dream to the same degree, and that the dream book does not contain only the first series of Poe's tales. On to it, as a matter of fact, are tagged the *Nouvelles Histoires extraordinaires*, whose contents (except for the preface) had all appeared previously in *Le Pays* along with the contents of the *Histoires*, and *Les Fleurs du Mal*.

In the *Histoires*, the only unpublished text, aside from *Le Scarabée d'or* (*The Gold Bug*), unpublished only in its translation by Baudelaire, is the new version of the study on 'Edgar Poe, sa vie et ses œuvres', of which, moreover, a fragment has appeared in *Le Pays* on February 25th.

Baudelaire calls attention to this novelty in the letter to his mother of March 15th, 1856, two days after the dream and its transcription; he announces the leaving with Ancelle of the volume dedicated to her, on the cover of which he has 'scribbled worthlessly':

'Read the introductory article – it is not the one you know. – Not fifty lines of the first one remain. – This one is written so as to produce violent reactions. – Moreover, I've succeeded pretty well – for I'm still attacked by young scamps from time to time.'

The separation into two volumes of these *Histoires*

corresponds first of all to a commercial intention on the publisher's part, but Baudelaire effects it in such a way that it serves a didactic plan based on the development of his relations with Edgar Poe.

The first volume is intended to 'attach' the second, as the whole series is to open the way for *Les Fleurs du Mal*. The entire publication is articulated as follows: the appearance of virtually the whole series of the *Histoires* in *Le Pays* precedes that of the eighteen poems entitled *Fleurs du Mal* for the first time in *La Revue des Deux Mondes* on June 1st, 1855. The publication of the second volume, the *Nouvelles Histoires extraordinaires*, will precede by several months that of the first edition of the poems in a volume on June 25th, 1857.

The transition from the first to the second volume reproduces Baudelaire's transition from a first Poe, the one whose 'Mesmeric Revelation' he translated in 1848, to a second one, in whom he is astounded to discover, at the end of 1851, ideas similar to those of Joseph de Maistre.

In the study on 'Edgar Poe, sa vie et ses œuvres' which appears as a preface to the *Histoires* on March 12th, 1856, Baudelaire forewarns his reader:

'If, as I hope, I have a further opportunity to speak of this poet, I shall give an analysis of his literary and philosophical opinions, as well as of the works whose complete translation would have little chance of success with a public greatly preferring diversion and emotion to the most important philosophic truths.'

In the hope of an article which never came, he had sent his work to Sainte-Beuve on March 19th, and followed it with a letter on the 26th, in which he explained with great exactitude the articulation of the three books, or more exactly of the four books, since he associated with the *Fleurs du Mal* their prose commentary:

'There will be a second volume and a second preface. The first volume is intended to attract the public: *Entertainments (Jongleries), speculation, hoaxes,* etc. ... 'Ligeia' is the only important piece that is morally linked with the second volume.

'The second volume is of a higher order of fantasy: *Hallucinations, mental diseases, pure grotesquery, supernaturalism,* etc. ...

'The second preface will contain the analysis of the works I shall not translate, in particular the discussion of the author's *literary* and *scientific* opinions ...

'The first preface, which you have seen, and in which I've tried to present a sharp protest against Americanism, is virtually complete from a biographical point of view. Many will pretend to regard Poe as merely an *entertainer (jongleur)*, but I shall scrupulously emphasize the supernatural character of his poetry and his tales. He is American only as an *entertainer*. As for the rest, his thought is virtually *anti-American*. Besides, he has ridiculed his compatriots as much as he could ...

'After the Poe will come two volumes of my own, one of critical articles, and the other of poems.'

(b) Entertainment

'Entertainments, speculation, hoaxes'; here is how the study on 'Edgar Poe, sa vie et ses œuvres' develops this characterization:

'I could introduce the reader into the mysteries of his fabrication, expatiate at length on the share of American genius that makes him delight in a difficulty overcome, a riddle explained, a *tour de force* achieved

– which encourages him to enjoy himself with an almost childish and almost perverse relish in the world of probabilities and conjectures, and to create *hoaxes* to which his subtle art has given a credible life. No one will deny that Poe is a marvellous entertainer …'

In a note added to the translation of 'The Un-paralleled Adventure of One Hans Pfaall' in *Le Pays* of April 20th, 1855, Baudelaire summarizes a text in which Poe compares his own narrative to other 'voyages to the moon':

'Here is Poe's conclusion, which is not without interest for those who enjoy peering about in the study of a man of genius – Jean-Paul's square sheets of paper skewered on wire – Balzac's arachnean *proofs* – Buffon's marginal notes, etc.

'In these various brochures, the aim is always satirical; the theme being a description of Lunarian customs as compared with ours. In none is there any effort at *plausibility* in the details of the voyage itself. The writers seem, in each instance, to be utterly uninformed in respect to astronomy. In 'Hans Pfaall' the design is original, at any rate as regards an attempt at *verisimilitude* in the application of scientific principles (so far as the whimsical nature of the subject would permit) to the actual passage between the earth and the moon.

'I grant that the reader may smile – I myself have more than once smiled upon surprising my author's typical foibles. Will not the pettiness of any great man always be a touching spectacle to an impartial mind? It is really remarkable to see a mind, at times so profoundly Germanic and at times so seriously oriental, betray at certain moments the Americanism with which it is saturated.'

But we must certainly not infer from this separation and from this hierarchy that Baudelaire rejects a part of Poe's work as mere entertainment or as pure Americanism, an error several of his contemporaries have committed. Already the 1852 study on 'Edgar Allan Poe, sa vie et ses ouvrages' declared:

'I should like to characterize Poe's work quite briefly and quite precisely, for it is an entirely new literary production. What stamps it with its essential character and distinguishes it from all others is, if I may be permitted these singular words, its speculativeness and its "probabilism".'

But most of all, in the 'Notes nouvelles sur Edgar Poe', Baudelaire will return to and defend this term 'entertainer' with a final energy:

'I must explain my terms with some care; for recently an indiscreet critic made use of the word *entertainer*, which I myself had applied to the noble poet almost as a eulogy, to denigrate Edgar Poe and to question the sincerity of my admiration ...

'Lastly, in order to confirm my thought in a still more explicit way, Poe was always great, not only in his noble conceptions, but even as a joker.'

(c) The anti-Franklin

Poe's American-ness, the fact that he was not an exile in America, an emigrant, but that he had, as far as was then possible, roots in America ('Mr Poe's family was one of the most respectable of Baltimore. His maternal grandfather had served as *quartermaster-general* in the War of Independence, and La Fayette regarded him with great esteem and friendship'), counts for a great deal in the attraction he exerts for Baudelaire, and must carry weight, according to the latter, with the French public.

There is, as a matter of fact, in this new country, despite all the symptoms of precocious senility that it reveals, an incontestable, thrilling modernity. Hence Baudelaire's fascination is constantly mixed with denigration, and if Poe is so great and so important, it is because his criticism of American life is not external to it, but because it is America turning against herself for the first time, refuting the hasty conclusions which a certain sector of the French bourgeoisie would like to draw from the spectacle it affords.

Entertainment is the very moment of this reversal. Poe carries certain characteristic features of the American much farther than any other writer among his compatriots, and it is when he does so that his work, without one's even being able to ask whether he intended it or not, constitutes the most violent criticism yet made of American life and its hypocrisy. Once this situation is established, taken note of, it is obvious that he will consciously, deliberately become critical, but his entire attack will be rooted in the very soil of this new country.

It is because Poe possesses to a higher degree than the majority of those around him certain of the qualities which the latter recognize as their own, that his genius becomes their caricature, and that they begin hating him, in whom those qualities of which they believed themselves certain are precisely the ones put in doubt. It is everything they think of themselves that such a man risks denouncing as a lie :

'In this swarm of mediocrities, in this world captivated by material improvements – a new kind of scandal that makes us realize the greatness of idle nations – in this society greedy for diversion, in love with life, but especially with a life full of excitements, a man appeared who was great not only by his metaphysical subtlety, by the sinister or ravishing beauty of his ideas, by the rigour of his analysis, but great too, and no less great, as *caricature*.'

In this 'society greedy for diversion, in love with life, but especially with a life full of excitements' we of course recognize a Baudelairian ideal, the one the poet will develop so admirably apropos of Constantin Guys in *Le Peintre de la vie moderne*. Would such a society not be the one to which the enterprise of *Les Paradis artificiels* ideally applies?

Poe, for Baudelaire, is the anti-Franklin not because he has qualities opposed to those of the illustrious inventor of the lightning-rod, but because in him these same qualities attain such a pitch that they reverse the situation:

'The author who in *The Colloquy of Monos and Una* releases the torrent of his scorn and disgust upon democracy, progress and *civilization* is the same author who, to ensure his countrymen's credulity and delight their idle tastes, has ingeniously fabricated the *hoaxes* most flattering to the pride of *modern man*. Seen in this light, Poe reminds me of a helot who wants to make his master blush.'

(d) The Indian

Poe's anti-Americanism sends its roots deep into this American-ness; his poetry, in the broad sense of the word, is based for Baudelaire not on the present American society but on the primitive American substratum, on the 'Savage', on the Indian, whence the apology for the latter, not as innocence but as a higher creature:

'If one wishes to compare modern man, civilized man, with the savage, or rather a so-called civilized nation with a so-called savage nation, that is, one

I

deprived of all the ingenious inventions that relieve the individual of heroism, who could fail to see that all the honours go to the savage? By this nature, by necessity even, he is encyclopaedic, while civilized man finds himself confined in the infinitely petty regions of specialization. Civilized man invents the philosophy of progress to console himself for his abdication and his decadence; while the savage, a feared and respected husband, a warrior compelled to exhibit personal bravery, a poet in the melancholy hours when the setting sun invites him to sing of the past and his ancestors, approaches closer to the ideal. What lacuna dare we reproach him for? He has a priest, a wizard and a physician. Indeed, he has the dandy, supreme incarnation of the idea of the beautiful in terms of material life, the man who dictates forms and arbitrates manners. His clothes, his adornments, his weapons, his calumet bear witness to an inventive faculty which has long since deserted us. Shall we compare our slothful eyes and our deadened ears to these eyes that pierce the fog, these ears that *hear the grass grow?* ... As for religion, I would not speak of Vitzili-poutzli as frivolously as Alfred de Musset has done; I confess without shame that I greatly prefer the cult of Teutatès to that of Mammon; and the priest who offers to the cruel extortioner of human offerings victims who die *honourably*, victims who *want* to die, seems to me a being quite gentle and humane compared to the financier who immolates populations to his own interest alone.'[1]

The American savage will become inseparable from Baudelaire's notion of dandyism as ersatz exterior and prefigurative sign of poetry. He returns to this twice

[1] The Aztec god Huitzilopochtli is presumably referred to here. I cannot identify Teutatès. – *Ed. note.*

in the chapter on the dandy in *Le Peintre de la vie moderne*:

'Dandyism is an institution ... that is, extremely widespread, since Chateaubriand has found it in the forests and beside the lakes of the New World.'

'Dandyism is the last flash of heroism in decadent societies; and the dandy rediscovered by the traveller in North America does not in the least invalidate this notion; for nothing keeps us from supposing that the tribes we call *savage* are the wreckage of great vanished civilizations.'

Edgar Poe, rebellious son of present-day America, receives the inheritance of these Indian dandies. Entertainment, or Americanism carried to its logical conclusion, opens a channel through which he receives, almost without realizing it, in an America of much greater depth, an anterior world across the sea.

(e) The book's obscenity

When Baudelaire, scandalized, reproaches present-day America for being captivated by material improvements, we must realize that he is not condemning these improvements as such. When he analysed *The Gold Bug* in the 1852 study, he praised Edgar Poe most for having described a material treasure:

'How beautiful the description of the treasure is, and what a splendid sensation of warmth and brilliance it gives us! For the treasure is found! *It was not a dream*, as is generally the case in all these novels where the author effects a brutal awakening after having excited the reader's mind by certain appetizing hopes; this time, it is a *real* treasure, and the decipherer has well deserved it ... The description of this wealth gives one a dizzying sense of greatness and philanthropic hankerings. In the chest buried by the pirate Kidd, there was certainly enough to solace many unknown despairs.'

In the famous entry in the Notebook, let us fix our attention on the first word in the list, given as the key to all that follows:

'Salvation is money, glory, security, the removal of the legal guardianship, Jeanne's life.'

He himself will celebrate, in *Le Peintre de la vie moderne*, those material improvements that permit man to transcend nature and realize poetry: stuffs, carriages, make-up, artificial light.

No, what Baudelaire holds against America is its making these material improvements into a screen to conceal the catastrophic consequences of what he considers as its fundamental error concerning human nature, that is, its pretension to virtue, its disregard of the universal and irresistible character of what it calls evil – an error, a disregard much more serious, much more deeply anchored than in France on account of America's initial puritanism, but which threaten France as well,

of what it calls evil and which is closely related to the magnificent savage and in particular to his sensuality.

The industrial new world Fourier described, instead of guaranteeing man his freedom, takes it from him, and pays him with illusory progress which serves only to conceal its failure.

Thus it is because the puritan fails to extinguish in himself the appeals of this evil, of this savage, of this sensuality and of this invention, that he proclaims so loudly his success in the realms of commercial production, and that he displays his money so ostentatiously. Industry, whose enormous merit is that it permits modernity, is also corrupted. This precious mask becomes a leprosy. What was to transcend nature no longer seeks anything more than to efface, to disfigure it.

We can imagine Baudelaire's emotion, living with Jeanne, following the metamorphoses of her face, when he read this passage from *The Colloquy of Monos and Una*, a fundamental text, for him, of Poe's anti-Americanism:

'The fair face of Nature was deformed as with the ravages of some loathsome disease.'

It is this denunciation of something that was to be kept hidden at all costs that constitutes in Baudelaire's eyes the Virginian's unique value:

'But here is the most important of all: we shall note that this author, the product of a self-infatuated age, child of a nation more self-infatuated than any other, has clearly seen, has imperturbably declared the natural wickedness of man',

a wickedness which in the French poet will assume, as we know, all the characteristics of another goodness.

Poe's life and work tear aside a veil, that veil with which America tries to cover itself before the European bourgeoisie and before its own as well. He exposes the divorce between this nation's appearance and its reality, merely by taking seriously certain of its own declarations, for it is precisely in the nation that unconditionally proclaimed all men equal that chained Negroes are burned, 'guilty of having felt their black cheeks flooded with the red of honour'; it is precisely in the nation claiming the people governs itself that a revolver is fired 'into the *parterre* of a theatre'; it is precisely in the nation of the puritans, that is, of those who affirm that sexuality can be

denied and assert that they make love only to pro-
create, that polygamy is established in 'the Western
paradises', and that the '*cure of nine-month diseases*'
is advertised on walls.

What the American appearance seems to promise
the bourgeoisie is a futile progress, the establishment
of its rule in ever greater comfort and security. What
the American reality actually announces, in the
mouth of Edgar Poe, is the stubborn persistence of that
generous, captivating, indomitable 'evil',

> Ô Prince de l'exil à qui l'on a fait tort,
> Et qui, vaincu, toujours se redresse plus fort,

this 'evil' that explodes in the transformation of
victim into executioner,

> Toi qui fais au proscrit ce regard calme et haut
> Qui damne tout un peuple autour d'un échafaud,

and in the merciful power of wine,

> Toi qui, magiquement, assouplis les vieux os
> De l'ivrogne attardé foulé par les chevaux,

this 'evil' to whose problem Baudelaire devotes all
his attention, all his life,
this 'evil' which cannot be the evil spoken of, the
evil they speak of.

Hence we understand why the book in the dream
'turns out to be' an obscene book, although

'what corroborates Mrs Frances Osgood's notion
concerning Poe's chivalrous respect for women is that
despite his prodigious talent for the grotesque and the
horrible, there is not, in his entire works, a single
passage that deals with lubricity or even with the
pleasure of the senses.'

Poe's work tears away a veil that all respectable

people are concerned to leave undisturbed, whether they are royalists, Bonapartists, or republicans; worse still, his work *is* the very veil which is being torn. Thus the *Histoires extraordinaires* are like a gaping garment through which the true Poe, and the profoundest America, show only, so to speak, the tips of their ears.

Baudelaire himself indicates to Sainte-Beuve – in the hope, of course, that the latter will pass on the information – the passage on the United States 'which counters all accepted notions' and the tale which is the closest to what will follow, 'Ligeia', in which the hero's life is inundated by an oneiric layer which he cannot master, on the occasion of his second marriage, in the preparation of the strange decor of the nuptial bedroom that will magically identify the second wife with the first, a tale obviously linked to the failure of Poe's second marriage, described in Baudelaire's essay.

Behind the *Histoires extraordinaires* are silhouetted the forthcoming *Fleurs du Mal*, which, of course, could much more easily be considered an obscene book, yet what the dream reveals is the close relationship between the most daring passages of *Les Fleurs du Mal* and the anti-American declarations of the 1856 study, considerably intensified and enlarged the following year in the 'Notes nouvelles'.

We see how naturally the night-time mind shifts from the book to the unbuttoned trousers.

11

THE SCHOOLBOYS

(a) The complaints of Hégésippe

'The day the young writer corrects his first proofs he
is as proud as the schoolboy who has just caught his
first dose of the clap.'

In the great brothel, Baudelaire finds himself a
schoolboy again, and with his timidity, his innocence
of the days before his disease, he joins the schoolboy
Poe.

In his autobiographical note, Baudelaire character-
izes his school years thus:

'Childhood: old Louis XVI furniture, antiques, Consulate, pastels, eighteenth-century society.

After 1830, Collège de Lyon, fights, quarrels with
teachers and classmates, severe fits of depression.

'Return to Paris, school and education by my stepfather (General Aupick).

'Youth: Expulsion from Louis Le Grand, business
of the baccalaureate.'

The word 'Consulate' already gives us a clue with
regard to the 'Egyptian figures' we shall find in the
halls of the dreams. Madame Aupick's house must
have had some 'home from Egypt' furnishings in it.

But, in particular, the whole passage is an impressive commentary on these strophes of the first poem
of Les Fleurs du Mal, that cruel poetic autobiography
called 'Bénédiction'.

After the anathemas of the infamous mother who
calls an infamous God to witness:

Je ferai rejaillir ta haine qui m'accable
Sur l'instrument maudit de tes méchancetés,
Et je tordrai si bien cet arbre misérable,
Qu'il ne pourra pousser ses boutons empestés!

come these lines:

Tous ceux qu'il veut aimer l'observent avec crainte.
Ou bien, s'enhardissant de sa tranquillité,
Cherchent à qui saura lui tirer une plainte,
Et font sur lui l'essai de leur férocité.

Dans le pain et le vin destinés à sa bouche
Ils mêlent de la cendre avec d'impurs crachats;
Avec hypocrisie ils jettent ce qu'il touche,
Et s'accusent d'avoir mis leurs pieds dans ses pas.

A martyr schoolboy, he must show his strength of
spirit by enduring all without complaint. He will
therefore have only scorn for a snivelling Hégésippe
Moreau. He will bitterly reproach the latter, in the
article he devotes to him, for complaining about his
schooldays, though they were less harsh than his own.

Un ogre, ayant flairé la chair qui vient de naître,
M'emporta, vagissant, dans sa robe de prêtre,
Et je grandis, captif, parmi ces écoliers,
Noirs frelons que Montrouge essaime par milliers.

'How really monstrous must this ogre (an ecclesias-
tic) be to carry off puling little Hégésippe in his
priest's robe, in his stinking and repulsive priest's robe
(soutane)! Cruel kidnapper! The word ogre implies a
determined taste for raw flesh; why, moreover, would
he have scented such flesh? And yet we see in the next
line that young Hégésippe hasn't been eaten, since on
the contrary he grows up (captive, it's true) like five
hundred other schoolmates the ogre hasn't eaten

either, and to whom he taught Latin, which will permit the martyr Hégésippe to write his own language a little less badly than all those who have not had the misfortune to be carried off by an *ogre*.'

For Baudelaire, the future poet is necessarily unhappy in school, but since his activity turns this unhappiness into a blessing he must not, cannot complain. By complaining, Hégésippe Moreau shows that he has not been so unhappy after all, that his misery has not gone far enough to make him a true poet.

Baudelaire himself, wanting to prove himself a poet, faces this contradiction : to reveal that he has been wretched during his schooldays, and reveal at the same time that he has been sufficiently virile not to complain about it.

This is why he speaks of the poet in general in 'Bénédiction'; this is why he drily lists facts in the autobiographical note. But the best solution will be given him by the reference to Edgar Poe.

Hégésippe Moreau merely wants to rouse sympathy, to re-enter his society by means of pity; Baudelaire and Poe want to destroy.

(b) 'William Wilson'

It is as early as Poe's schooldays that he will present himself to Baudelaire as an ideal alter ego. In the *Histoires* and the *Nouvelles Histoires* there are many examples of doubles; there is in particular a story of doubles at school : 'William Wilson'.

The hero of this tale has a friend who resembles him like a brother, or more exactly, like an image in a mirror. Baudelaire here recognizes the reflection of the young Poe, recognizes himself in this reflection. He can henceforth show how Poe has been miserable in school, and further, how brave he has been because he has not complained of it; Baudelaire has merely complained for him.

It is in the 1852 study that we find this meditation on Poe's childhood, on his schooldays in England:

'The character, the genius, the style of a man is formed by the apparently commonplace circumstances of his earliest youth. If all the men who have held the world's stage had written down their childhood impressions, what an excellent psychological dictionary we should possess! The colours of Edgar Poe's sensibility stand out violently against the background of American literature. His compatriots find him scarcely American at all, and yet he is not English. It is therefore a piece of good luck to be able to include in these tales a little-known story, "William Wilson", a singular narrative of his life at the school of Stoke Newington. All of Edgar Poe's tales are biographical in a sense. One finds the man in the work. The characters and the incidents are the frame and the drapery of his memories.'

Baudelaire then quotes a long passage from 'William Wilson', from which I shall retain only what leads directly to the commentary with which he accompanies it:

'The school-room was the largest in the house – I could not help thinking, in the world. It was very long, narrow, and dismally low, with pointed Gothic windows and a ceiling of oak. In a remote and terror-inspiring angle was a square enclosure of eight or ten feet, comprising the *sanctum*, 'during hours', of our principal, the Reverend Dr Bransby. It was a solid structure, with massy door, sooner than open which in the absence of the 'Dominie', we would all have willingly perished by the *peine forte et dure*. In other angles were two other similar boxes, far less reverenced, indeed, but still greatly matters of awe. One of these was the pulpit of the "classical" usher, one of the "English and mathematical". Interspersed about the room, crossing and recrossing in endless irregularity, were innumerable benches and desks, black, ancient and time-worn, piled desperately with much-bethumbed books, and so beseamed with initial letters, names at full length, grotesque figures and other multiplied efforts of the knife, as to have entirely lost what little of original form might have been their portion in days long departed. A huge bucket with water stood at one extremity of the room, and a clock of stupendous dimensions at the other.

'Encompassed by the massy walls of this venerable academy, I passed, yet not in tedium or disgust, the years of the third lustrum of my life. The teeming brain of childhood requires no external world of incident to occupy or amuse it; and the apparently dismal monotony of a school was replete with more intense excitement than my riper youth has derived from luxury, or my full manhood from crime. Yet I must believe that my first mental development had in it much of the uncommon – and even of the *outré*. Upon mankind at large the events of very early existence rarely leave in mature age any definite impression. All is grey shadow – a weak and irregular remembrance – an indistinct regathering of feeble pleasures and phantasmagoric pains. With me this is not so. In childhood I must have felt with the energy of a man what I now find stamped upon memory in lines as vivid, as deep, and as durable as the *exergues* of the Carthaginian medals.

'Yet in fact – in the fact of the world's view – how little was there to remember! The morning's awakening, the nightly summons to bed; the connings, the recitations; the periodical half-holidays, and perambulations; the play-ground, with its broils, its pastimes, its intrigues; – these, by a mental sorcery long forgotten, were made to involve a wilderness of sensation, a world of rich incident, an universe of varied emotion, of excitement the most passionate and spirit-stirring. *"Oh, le bon temps, que ce siècle de fer!"* '

Whereas Poe seems quite pleased with the school of Stoke Newington, Baudelaire emphasizes its horror, and of course marvels at his model's impassivity.

'What do you say about this fragment? Does not the character of this singular man already reveal itself somewhat? For myself, I feel this school scene steeped in a kind of black perfume. I feel the shudder of the first years of claustration circulating in it. The hours of confinement, the discomfort of frightened and abandoned childhood, the terror of the master our enemy, the hatred of tyrannical schoolmates, the solitude of the heart, all these tortures of youth Poe has not suffered. So many subjects for melancholy have not vanquished him. Young, he loves solitude, or rather, he does not feel alone; he loves his passions. *The teeming brain of childhood* renders everything pleasant, illuminates everything. We see already how the exercise of the will and solitary pride will play a great role in his life. And would one not say that he enjoys suffering, that he anticipates this future inseparable companion of his life, and that he summons it with a lustful severity, like a young gladiator? The poor child has neither father nor mother, but he is happy: he glorifies himself upon being profoundly marked.'

Of course, Baudelaire himself had suffered 'the hours of confinement, the discomfort of frightened and abandoned childhood, the terror of the master our enemy, the hatred of tyrannical schoolmates, the solitude of the heart, all these tortures of youth' to their fullest extent; and yet, in him too, the teeming brain of childhood ('genius is only *childhood rediscovered* at will, childhood now endowed, in order to express itself, with virile organs and with the analytic spirit … ') illuminated everything.

Hence, in the poem 'Bénédiction':

Pourtant, sous la tutelle invisible d'un ange,
L'enfant déshérité s'enivre de soleil,
Et dans tout ce qu'il boit et dans tout ce qu'il mange
Retrouve l'ambroisie et le nectar vermeil.

Il joue avec le vent, cause avec le nuage,
Et s'enivre en chantant du chemin de la croix;
Et l'Esprit qui le suit dans son pèlerinage
Pleure de le voir gai comme un oiseau des bois.

12

THE MUSEUM

(a) The school-brothel

In the 'enormous, interconnecting halls – badly lit, their atmosphere melancholy and faded' of the huge brothel, we have no difficulty recognizing the Stoke Newington school. In the preceding chapter, I have followed the text of the 1852 study; I shall now quote from the one that appeared serially in *Le Pays* and which will be reprinted in the *Nouvelles Histoires extraordinaires*:

'But the house! – how quaint an old building was this! – to me how veritably a place of enchantment! There was really no end to its windings – to its incomprehensible subdivisions. It was difficult, at any given time, to say with certainty upon which of its two stories one happened to be. From each room to every other there were sure to be found three or four steps either in ascent or descent. Then the lateral branches were innumerable – inconceivable – and so returning in upon themselves, that our most exact ideas in regard to the whole mansion were not very far different from those with which we pondered upon infinity. During the five years of my residence here, I was never able to ascertain with precision, in what remote locality lay the little sleeping apartment assigned to myself and some eighteen or twenty other scholars.'

In the 1852 study, Baudelaire adds to his translation of this last sentence the following precious note:

'Habitual hallucination of the eyes of childhood, which magnify and complicate objects.'

The whores in the dream are scattered through these galleries like the school desks in the study hall. The carvings on the desks form a little museum, masterpieces of the knife, grotesque figures, whole names ('images of bizarre, monstrous, almost shapeless creatures, like meteorites. In a corner of each drawing, here is a note ... '), and, to emphasize the resemblance, the schoolboy Baudelaire 'will scribble worthlessly' on the copy of the *Histoires* that he will set aside for his mother.

(b) The museum-bedroom

The school-brothel is thus a museum.

For a long time, for Baudelaire, galleries, in the sense of picture galleries, particularly the Louvre Museum, were places of assignation, as this letter to his mother of December 16th, 1847, indicates:

'I wanted to ask you to meet me at *the Louvre* to-day, *in the big Salon Carré*, whenever is convenient for you, but as early as you can. Besides, the Museum isn't open before eleven. It's the best place in Paris to talk; it's heated, you can wait there without getting bored, and besides, it's the most acceptable meeting-place for a woman.'

It's a whore herself who reveals the Louvre to Baudelaire as a kind of super-brothel, as this note for *Mon cœur mis à nu* indicates:

'All the bourgeois idiots who keep muttering about immorality in art and other nonsense remind me of Louise Villedieu, a five-franc whore who once went with me to the Louvre, where she had never been, and began blushing, covering her face, and tugging me by the sleeve every other minute, asking me, in front of the statues and the immortal paintings, how such obscenities could be shown in public.'

Baudelaire has often spoken of Poe as a painter, and of his tales as scenes. Hence, in *Le Peintre de la vie moderne* :

'Do you remember a scene (and it really is a scene!) described by the most powerful pen of the age and which is called "The Man of the Crowd"?'

Within the tales themselves, we find many examples of museums, especially in 'Berenice' :

'Our line has been called a race of visionaries; and in many striking particulars – in the character of the family mansion – in the frescoes of the chief saloon – in the tapestries of the dormitories – in the chiselling of some buttresses in the armoury – but more especially in the gallery of antique paintings – in the fashion of the library chamber – and, lastly, in the very peculiar nature of the library's contents, there is more than sufficient evidence to warrant the belief.

'The recollections of my earliest years are connected with that chamber, and with its volumes – of which latter I will say no more. Here died my mother. Herein was I born.'

In our dream :

'a monster born in the house and that stays eternally on a pedestal. Although alive, it is therefore part of the museum.'

(c) 'Ligeia'

But we shall find this museum-bedroom described much more amply in the very tale Baudelaire told Sainte-Beuve was the only one in the first volume that truly revealed the depths of the second, 'Ligeia', where it will constitute the very pivot of the incident, since it permits the hero to identify his second marriage with the first.

After the death of his first wife, Ligeia, the narrator takes up residence in England and, unconsciously inspired by the dead woman, assembles for his second wedding night a singular bedroom, instrument of a magical operation by which Ligeia will be reborn in the body of the woman supposed to succeed her :

'There is no individual portion of the architecture and decoration of that bridal chamber which is not now visibly before me. Where were the souls of the haughty family of the bride, when, through thirst of gold, they permitted to pass the threshold of an apartment so bedecked, a maiden and a daughter so beloved? ...

'Some few ottomans and golden candelabra, of Eastern figure, were in various stations about – and there was the couch, too – the bridal couch – of an Indian model, and low, and sculptured of solid ebony, with a pall-like canopy above. In each of the angles of the chamber stood on end a gigantic sarcophagus of black granite, from the tombs of the kings over against Luxor, with their aged lids full of immemorial sculpture. But in the draping of the apartment lay, alas! the chief phantasy of all. The lofty walls, gigantic in height – even unproportionably so – were hung from summit to foot, in vast folds, with a heavy and massive-looking tapestry – tapestry of a material which was found alike as a carpet on the floor, as a covering for the ottomans and the ebony bed, as a canopy for the bed, and as the gorgeous volutes of the curtains which partially shaded the window. The material was the richest cloth of gold. It was spotted all over, at irregular intervals, with arabesque figures, about a foot in diameter, and wrought upon the cloth

146

in patterns of the most jetty black. But these figures partook of the true character of the arabesque only when regarded from a single point of view. By a contrivance now common, and indeed traceable to a very remote period of antiquity, they were made changeable in aspect. To one entering the room, they bore the appearance of simple monstrosities; but upon a farther advance, this appearance gradually departed; and step by step, as the visitor moved his station in the chamber, he saw himself surrounded by an endless succession of the ghastly forms which belong to the superstition of the Norman, or arise in the guilty slumbers of the monk ... '

Could Edgar Poe have seen, during his years at Stoke Newington, in the collection of the Earls of Radnor, Holbein's 'Ambassadors'?

(d) 'Le Siècle'

But apropos of museums, let us remember:

'There is really only one newspaper in the world – *Le Siècle* – stupid enough to open a house of prostitution and install a kind of medical museum in it at the same time. In fact, I suddenly decide, it is *Le Siècle* which has raised the money for this brothel scheme, and the medical museum is explained by the paper's mania for progress, *science, dissemination of knowledge.*'

Does not the bitter resentment against *Le Siècle* also proceed from a disappointment?

As a matter of fact, a letter of March 17th, 1854, to Eugène Pelletan informs us that Baudelaire had offered him the *Histoires extraordinaires* for the second feuilleton of his paper, entitled 'Musée littéraire'.

The museum into which we emerge is therefore Madame Aupick's bedroom with its Consulate furnishings, but already haunted in advance by the entire works of Edgar Poe, 'that extremely individual genius, that unique temperament which has permitted him to paint and to explain, in an impeccable, thrilling, terrible manner, *the exception in the moral order.*'

And the person born in this bedroom is himself a Poe character, or more exactly risks being only a Poe character if he doesn't manage to imitate Poe himself.

'Poe's characters, or rather Poe's character, the man with intensely sensitive faculties, the man with exhausted nerves, the man whose patient and ardent will flings defiance at life's difficulties, the man whose gaze is strained with the intensity of a drawn sword on objects that grow larger as he stares at them – is Poe himself.' It was Baudelaire himself. 'Although alive, it is therefore part of the museum.'

In the middle of this room, his sinister image, that image which in fact the publication of the *Histoires* may permit him to avoid resembling but which subsists as a threat, a sword of Damocles over his head, will gradually become clearer.

13

THE BIRDS

(a) Albatross and penguins

Meteorites are discussed in 'The Unparalleled Adventure of One Hans Pfaall'; as for the birds, we know that they have an important place in the *Narrative of A. Gordon Pym*. Baudelaire admits that Chapter xiv of this work has been particularly difficult to translate. In it, Poe describes the penguin as a veritable dandy among birds, astonishingly similar to man :

'The royal penguin, so called from its size and beautiful plumage, is the largest. The upper part of the body is usually grey, sometimes of a lilac tint; the under portion of the purest white imaginable. The head is of a glossy and most brilliant black, the feet also. The chief beauty of the plumage, however, consists in two broad stripes of a gold colour, which pass along from the head to the breast. The bill is long, and either pink or bright scarlet. These birds walk erect, with a stately carriage. They carry their heads high with their wings dropping like two arms, and, as their tails project from their body in a line with the legs, the resemblance to a human figure is very striking, and would be apt to deceive the spectator at a casual glance or in the gloom of the evening.'

He then describes the albatross as linked with the penguin by a remarkable symbiosis, which can only remind us, as it reminds him, of the relation of the poet to the dandy :

'The albatross is one of the largest and fiercest of
the South Sea birds. It is of the gull species, and takes
its prey on the wing, never coming to land except for
the purpose of breeding. Between this bird and the
penguin the most singular friendship exists. Their
nests are constructed with great uniformity upon a
plan concerted between the two species – that of the
albatross being placed in the centre of a little square
formed by the nest of four penguins.'

Between the four sarcophagi of the bedroom in
'Ligeia' the little monster's egg will hatch.

Further, the raven is Poe's totemic animal, and
Baudelaire translates the word 'hoax' as *canard* (duck).
The first volume of the *Histoires*, according to the
letter to Sainte-Beuve, consists largely of *canards*, and
the *canard* is one of the most characteristic of Poe's
external qualities, one of the major features of his
garb.

(b) The living eye

The living eyes of the bird-pictures in the dream refer
us directly to one of the tales in the second volume,
The Tell-Tale Heart, one of the most important for
Baudelaire, since it is an illustration of the imp of
the perverse, or of the notion of evil as inspiration :

'I loved the old man. He had never wronged me.
He had never given me insult. For his gold I had no
desire. I think it was his eye! yes, it was this! He had
the eye of a vulture – a pale blue eye, with a film
over it. Whenever it fell upon me, my blood ran cold;
and so by degrees – very gradually – I made up my
mind to take the life of the old man, and thus rid myself of the eye for ever.'

'The Black Cat' offers illustration of the same
theme :

'In the next instant, a dozen stout arms were toiling at the wall. It fell bodily. The corpse, already greatly decayed and clotted with gore, stood erect before the eyes of the spectators. Upon its head, with red extended mouth and solitary eye of fire, sat the hideous beast whose craft had seduced me into murder, and whose informing voice had consigned me to the hangman.'

The living eye, the eye that is still alive in a corpse, is the unimpeachable sign, in Poe, that this 'mesmeric' underworld is on the point of being revealed. Read, for instance, the last lines of 'Ligeia':

'Shrinking from my touch, she let fall from her head, unloosened, the ghastly cerements which had confined it, and there streamed forth, into the rushing atmosphere of the chamber, huge masses of long and dishevelled hair; *it was blacker than the raven wings of the midnight!* And now slowly opened *the eyes* of the figure which stood before me. "Here then, at least," I shrieked aloud, "can I never – can I never be mistaken – these are the full, and the black, and the wild eyes – of my lost love – of the lady – of the LADY LIGEIA!"'

In 'The Facts in the Case of M. Valdemar', the death of the mesmerized patient, his passage to the other world, is expressed by the rolling of his eyes in their sockets, and the first sign of the awakening of the corpse is a 'partial descent of the iris'.

The same sign appears in 'Some Words with a Mummy':

'My eyes, happening to fall upon those of the Mummy, were there immediately riveted in amazement. My brief glance, in fact, had sufficed to assure me that the orbs which we had all supposed to be glass, and which were originally noticeable for a certain wild stare, were now so far covered by the lids, that only a small portion of the *tunica albuginea* remained visible.'

(c) A printer's error

But the theme of the birds is, as we know, much more important in Baudelaire himself than in his model. In *La Fanfarlo*, under the pseudonym of Manuela de Monteverde, Samuel Cramer, our poet's pseudonym, has published a collection of verse with the title *Les Orfraies* (*The Ospreys*). One of the earliest poems of *Les Fleurs du Mal* is called 'Les Hiboux' (The Owls):

> Ainsi que les dieux étrangers,
> Dardant leur œil rouge. Ils méditent.

In 1852, a review was planned of which Baudelaire was to be the editor and whose name was to be *Le Hibou philosophe* (*The Philosophical Owl*).

Lastly, we know that certain of the most famous poems abound in references to birds:

'Bénédiction' :

> Comme un tout jeune oiseau qui tremble et qui palpite,
> J'arracherai ce cœur tout rouge de son sein … ,

'Élévation' :

> Celui dont les pensers comme des alouettes,
> Vers les cieux du matin prennent un libre essor …

'Le Cygne',

'Un voyage a Cythère' :

> Mon cœur, comme un oiseau …

Mais voilà qu'en rasant la côte d'assez près
Pour troubler les oiseaux avec nos voiles blanches ...

De féroces oiseaux perchés sur leur pâture ...

Et ses bourreaux, gorgés de hideuses délices,
L'avaient à coups de bec absolument châtré ...

Devant toi, pauvre diable au souvenir si cher,
J'ai senti tous les becs et toutes les mâchoires
Des corbeaux lancinants et des panthères noires
Qui jadis aimaient tant à triturer ma chair ...

We must relate such consistency to Baudelaire's
own name. I know what a child can endure by way
of jokes about his name.[1] Where our poet is concerned,
let us recall his outrage when a printer's error transformed Baudelaire into Beaudelaire. On this account
he had the entire edition of his first translation of Poe's
'Philosophy of Furniture' destroyed.

I referred to the penguin above as a dandy among
birds. Translate this expression into the language of
the late eighteenth or early nineteenth century and
you get 'le beau de l'air'.

This pun, which may seem a little far-fetched to the
present-day reader, was then quite classical, as a
curious sequence of caricatures will show.

In Le Rabelais for July 25th, 1857, appears a picture in the series 'Odyssey of Pilou, fusilier in the 73rd
of the line', representing an unmade bed out of which
stick two straight legs. It is reprinted almost exactly
in a lithograph by Gillot, published on July 15th, 1858,
in the Journal inutile, with the caption 'Oh! c'est beau
de l'air'; and we find it again in the specimen number
of Le Boulevard for December 1st, 1861, embellished

[1] In French, Butor means 'bittern', and, by extension,
'booby'. – Tr. note.

this time with various accessories and 'gothic' shadows, under the title 'Les Nuits de Monsieur Baudelaire', and accompanied by a text by Théodore de Banville.

(d) *Leaving Virginia*

Lastly, two months before the dream, Baudelaire's attention had been attracted once more to the world of birds by Alphonse Toussenel's book *Ornithologie passionnelle*.

If the penguin, according to Poe's description, appears in the figure of the dandy, the albatross is the image of the poet:

> Le Poète est semblable au prince des nuées
> Qui hante la tempête et se rit de l'archer;
> Exilé sur le sol au milieu des huées,
> Ses ailes de géant l'empêchent de marcher.

This familiar poem, which comes second in the second edition of *Les Fleurs du Mal*, does not appear in the first. It was published for the first time, without the third strophe, with 'Le Voyage', in a brochure of only five or six copies in 1859. Yet three different accounts assure us that it is based on a real incident in the poet's life that occurred in 1848, during his return from Mauritius, that 'île de France' where Bernardin de Saint-Pierre had situated the adventures of his two innocent lovers.

The recollection of such an episode, its possibility as a poem, underlying our dream, link the bird-monsters to the tottering monster.

(e) Bird language

The bird announces the poet, the poet is a superior bird, but if he remains on the level of the bird, he will never be a true poet. Here again we have the image of what prefigures publication, but which is also suppressed by publication.

Hence we will not be surprised to rediscover this theme in Baudelaire's remarks on the man who for him is virtually the type of the false poet, i.e. Hégésippe Moreau:

'We know those sloth-abetting theories, based solely on metaphors, which permit the poet to regard himself as a chattering, frivolous, irresponsible, uncapturable bird, shifting his domicile from one branch to another.'

The bird of evil omen – owl, raven – will gradually become the very image of the man who has failed to be a poet, the man whose language, which was intended to be celestial, is reduced to croaking.

Hence when Baudelaire notices that despite all his efforts his activity contaminates and causes the unjust punishment of those who help him (I refer in particular to the condemnation of Poulet-Malassis for the publication of *Les Épaves*), in despair over his human language, he will no longer be willing to express himself save in that bird's language which was the promise of the former.

Hence, in the remote gallery, what we are shown is already the threat of the disease from which the publication of the *Histoires* seemed to have saved him for ever.

An impressive premonition, for see how Mairobert, in his article in *Le Figaro* for July 19th, 1866, under the title 'Pro and Con' describes our little monster:

'His face has changed by the growth of a completely grey beard – he had always been clean-shaven – and by the tanned look of the skull, which he leaves exposed to the July sun without appearing to suffer thereby. Paralysis has struck one eye, which no longer sees, and the tongue, which at certain painful moments – those of the showers, for instance – articulates with effort a little stream of oaths, something like the classical "sacré nom!" '

The incomparably loyal Asselineau, in a letter to Poulet-Malassis, will give him these details as to this language:

'Baudelaire seems to be quite comfortable in his sanatorium.

'He says four new words:

'*Bonjour, monsieur, Bonsoir*, monsieur, *Adieu*, and the name of his doctor. The said doctor glories in this victory which doesn't seem so splendid to me. Just because he's succeeded in making Baudelaire say a few words more doesn't mean that much progress has been made. It's evident that, once cured, he would talk; but all he will say as long as he's sick is merely parrot talk.

'Will he recover? That's the question. He himself doesn't seem to have many illusions about it, and from time to time he drops a few mournful *sacré noms* that are terrible to hear ... '

14

PINK AND GREEN

(a) The colours of the dawn

The hours have passed in the dream. The waking approaches, and the first light of dawn. What is surprising, then, if the figure of the little monster is 'of an Eastern colour', and if

> L'aurore grelottante en robe rose et verte

tinges it with the shades of her costume.

This dawn is hope, of course, but not merely hope – she is shivering, she is a 'Muse malade':

> Ma pauvre muse, hélas! qu'as-tu donc ce matin?
> Tes yeux creux sont peuplés de visions nocturnes,
> Et je vois tour à tour réfléchis sur son teint
> La folie et l'horreur froides et taciturnes.
>
> Le succube verdâtre et le rose lutin
> T'ont-ils versé la peur et l'amour de leurs urnes? ...

(b) The colours of the elect

In this light of dawn which he will have to abandon for

'Phoebus, and great Pan, the lord of harvests', for this noon and this extreme west, this evening twilight which he will celebrate so splendidly in his 'Notes nouvelles sur Edgar Poe':

'This sun that, a few hours ago, crushed all things

under its direct white light, will soon flood the western horizon with mingled colours. In the play of this dying sun, certain poetic spirits will find new delights; they will discover sparkling colonnades, cascades of molten metal, paradises of fire, a mournful splendour, the pleasure of regret, all the magic of dreams, all the memories of opium. And the sunset will appear to them, indeed, as a marvellous allegory of a soul imbued with life which descends behind the horizon with a magnificent store of thoughts and dreams',

the little monster is the budding poet, the poet who has not yet created himself, this child whom the adult considers with detachment, at whom he can even laugh, but his colours are those of his vocation, or, if we prefer, of his damnation : the mind enjoys the pun, and in our letter transcribing the dream there is a word designated only by its initial, a separate consonant which, like the sharp sign beside the musical clef, spans the entire narrative to attach itself to these designations of colour and translate them for us :

'There is in him much prose and verse.'[1]

(c) The colours of the Indian

In the chapter on colour in the *Salon de 1846*, a first description of the twilight linked these two tints :

'When the great crucible descends into the waters, red fanfares explode on all sides : a blood-red harmony floods the horizon, and the green turns a rich purple. But soon great throbbing blue shadows drive before them the host of tender pinks and oranges that seem to be the distant and diluted echo of the light ...'

[1] 'Il y a en lui beaucoup de prose [p/rose] et de vers.' *Vert*, the French word for green, is pronounced the same as the word for verse. – *Tr. note.*

A few lines later, this fundamental harmony perceived in the evening sky is pursued in the detail of
the human body :

' ... in the woman's reddish, bony and fine-skinned
hand we see that there is a perfect harmony between
the green of the strong veins that traverse it and the
sanguine tones that mark the joints; the pink nails
cut across the first joint that has various grey and
brown tones in it. As for the palm, the pinker, almost
purplish lines of life are separated from each other by
the system of green or blue veins that cross them.'

It is apparent that some effort is required to adjust
his description to his theory of colours : 'the red sings
the glory of the green', for it is difficult to grant that
the veins of the hand appear to us as green. It will
also be noticed that his pink inclines towards red.

But he finds this opposition of red and green ('for a
long time, opposite my window, there has been a
cabaret painted green and bright red, a delicious torment for my eyes'), 'singing' not only on hands, but
on faces as well in the canvases of the admirable
painter and ethnographer of the American prairies,
George Catlin.

'Monsieur Catlin has been particularly successful in
rendering the proud, free character and the noble expression of these splendid people; the formation of
their skulls is perfectly understood. By their relaxed
postures and the ease of their movements, these savages
permit us to understand antique sculpture. As for the
colour, it has something mysterious about it that
delights me more than I can say. The red – colour of
blood, colour of life – was so abundant in this dark
museum that it became an intoxication. As for the
landscapes, wooded mountains, huge savannas, solitary rivers, they were monotonously, eternally green;

red, a colour so baffling, so dense, more difficult to penetrate than a snake's eyes, and green, the calm, cheerful colour of smiling nature – I rediscover them both singing their melodic antithesis even on the countenance of these two heroes.'

We see how old the theme of the *beau sauvage américain* is for Baudelaire, predating his discovery of Poe, who will be grafted upon this stock. When Baudelaire, in the *Salon de 1859*, wants to praise Fromentin for having discovered dandyism in the Sahara, it is to Catlin's *Ioways* that he will continue to refer :[1]

'It is not only brilliant stuffs and curiously worked weapons that his eyes are attracted by, but particularly that gravity and that patrician dandyism which characterize the chiefs of the powerful tribes. Thus appeared to us, some fourteen years ago, those savages of North America, brought here by the painter Catlin, who even in their state of decadence made us dream of the art of Phidias and the grandeurs of Homer.'

In the bedroom-museum, obsessed by Poe's works, it is an American baby that Madame Aupick (then Baudelaire) has unwittingly produced.

[1] One surmises that these are the Iowa Indians. – *Ed. note.*

15

THE ROPE

(a) *The appendage*

Confronted with this blackish something, a kind of thick serpent, elastic as rubber, particularly considering the sharp sign governing the entire tonality of the dream through the initial P, the reader will probably have a translation ready, a translation which many texts by Poe or by Baudelaire corroborate.

As a matter of fact, in one of the *Nouvelles Histoires extraordinaires*, 'Lionizing', the nose evidently designates this other organ:

'I turned up my nose, and I spoke of myself.

' "Marvellous clever man!" said the Prince.

' "Superb!" said his guest; – and the next morning her Grace of Bless-my-Soul paid me a visit.

' "Will you go to Almack's, pretty creature?" she said, tapping me under the chin.

' "Upon honour," said I.

' "Nose and all?" she asked.

' "As I live," I replied.

' "Here then is a card, my life. Shall I say you *will* be there?"

' "Dear Duchess, with all my heart."

' "Pshaw, no! – but with all your nose?"

' "Every bit of it, my love," said I : – so I gave it a twist or two, and found myself at Almack's.

'The rooms were crowded to suffocation.

' "He is coming!" said somebody on the staircase.

' "He is coming!" said somebody farther up.

' "He is coming!" said somebody farther still.

' "He is come!" exclaimed the Duchess ... "He is come, the little love!" – and, seizing me firmly by both hands, she kissed me thrice upon the nose.

'A marked sensation immediately ensued.'

As for Baudelaire himself, in the prose-poem 'Les Tentations', for instance, he will wind around the purple tunic of the sexually ambiguous Eros Satan, 'in the manner of a sash, an iridescent serpent, which raised its head and languorously turned towards him its glowing eyes' – a character linked all the more closely to our little monster since he too totters, for 'at his delicate ankles dragged several links of a broken gold chain, and when the resulting awkwardness forced him to lower his eyes to the ground ... '

But we must at least notice that for this poor little monster this appendage is only a problem. Surrounded by whores, he can do nothing with them.

> Ses ailes de géant l'empêchent de marcher.

(b) The guide-rope and the gallows

Now if we re-read the *Histoires* and *Nouvelles Histoires* we shall find superimposed on this sensual image another image linked to the themes of suicide and aphasia. Our little monster drags with him the rope that can strangle him.

A dwarf, a dwarf who has difficulty in walking, is Poe's Hop-Frog who, 'through the distortion of his legs, could move only with great pain and difficulty along a road or floor', and who will use the chandelier chain as the instrument of his vengeance, transforming the king and his seven ministers into monkeys, then into living torches.

A dwarf carried along in a balloon the shape of a dunce's cap is Poe's Hans Pfaall who 'could not have been more than two feet in height', whose nose was 'prodigiously long, crooked, and inflammatory'.

If we want a more likely balloon, we need only refer to the tale which Baudelaire has placed just before 'The Unparalleled Adventure of One Hans Pfaall', 'The Balloon Hoax', in which we shall find the minute description of a rope that keeps the apparatus from rising :

'The balloon is furnished besides with a grapnel, and a guide-rope; which latter is of the most indispensable importance. A few words, in explanation, will here be necessary for such of our readers as are not conversant with the details of aërostation ...

'The guide-rope remedies the difficulty in the simplest manner conceivable. It is merely a very long rope which is suffered to trail from the car, and the effect of which is to prevent the balloon from changing its level in any material degree. If, for example, there should be a deposition of moisture upon the silk, and the machine begins to descend in consequence, there will be no necessity for discharging ballast to remedy the increase of weight, for it is remedied, or counteracted, in an exactly just proportion, by the deposit on the ground of just so much of the end of the rope as is necessary. If, on the other hand, any circumstances should cause undue levity, and consequent ascent, this levity is immediately counteracted by the additional weight of rope upraised from the earth. Thus, the balloon can neither ascend nor descend, except within very narrow limits, and its resources, either in gas or ballast, remain comparatively unimpaired.'

This moderating rope, which circumvents jolts and

keeps the balloon from changing its level, will become a murderous rope in 'The Black Cat'.

'What Parisian author who is even halfway well-read has not read "The Black Cat"?' Baudelaire asked in the 1852 study. He summarizes the tale and quotes a passage, precisely that of the hanging of the cat:

'*In the meantime the cat slowly recovered. The socket of the lost eye presented, it is true, a frightful appearance, but he no longer appeared to suffer any pain. He went about the house as usual, but, as might be expected, fled in extreme terror at my approach. I had so much of my old heart left, as to be at first grieved by this evident dislike on the part of a creature which had once so loved me ...*

'*One morning, in cold blood, I slipped a noose about its neck and hung it to the limb of a tree – hung it with the tears streaming from my eyes ...*'

In the remainder of the tale, the ghost of the hanged cat appears, during the burning of the narrator's house on the very evening of his crime. A single wall had partially resisted the fire's action: I now cite the text of the *Nouvelles Histoires*.

'About this wall a dense crowd were collected, and many persons seemed to be examining a particular portion of it with very minute and eager attention. The words "strange!" "singular!" and other similar expressions, excited my curiosity. I approached and saw, as if graven in bas-relief upon the white surface, the figure of a gigantic *cat*. The impression was given with an accuracy truly marvellous. There was a rope about the animal's neck.'

A little later, the narrator will find and adopt a new black cat, exactly like the preceding one save in regard to one detail: 'a large, although indefinite, splotch of white, covering nearly the whole region of the breast', a splotch which will not remain indefinite, which will gradually assume 'a rigorous distinctness of outline'.

'It was now the representation of an object that I shudder to name – and for this, above all, I loathed, and dreaded, and would have rid myself of the monster *had I dared* – it was now, I say, the image of a hideous – of a ghastly thing – of the GALLOWS! ... '

Hence, in 'Un voyage à Cythère' :

Dans ton île, ô Vénus! je n'ai trouvé debout
Qu'un gibet symbolique où pendait mon image ...

(c) *Gérard de Nerval*

And it will be remembered that in the introduction to the book published on Wednesday, March 12th, 1856, in this new version of the study on Edgar Poe, there is a discussion of an illustrious hanged man, the very man, in fact, whose *Voyage en Orient* had inspired the poem just quoted, and that Baudelaire had been careful to date his text on the anniversary of this great poet's death :

'Who does not remember the Parisian declamations upon Balzac's death, however suitably he died? And still more recently – exactly a year ago this January 26th – when a writer of an admirable frankness, of a high intelligence, and *who was always lucid*, discreetly, without bothering anyone – so discreetly that his discretion resembled contempt – gave up his soul in the darkest street he could find – what disgusting homilies! – what refined murder!'

Thus the publication of the *Histoires* is also the commemoration of Gérard de Nerval's suicide. Suicide, or quasi-suicide, super-suicide as in the case of

Edgar Poe? The expression 'what refined murder' already suggests the ambiguity of this death, and this question will obsess Baudelaire to the end of his lucid life, until he himself is strangled by this rope he dragged about.

Here we must give the affecting testimony of Catulle Mendès, who one night, probably in 1865, let Baudelaire sleep in his room. There occurred a long conversation in the darkness, concluding thus:

'Suddenly, but in a low, almost whispering voice, a voice of trust: "Did you know Gérard de Nerval?" "No," I answered. He continued: "He wasn't mad. Talk to Asselineau about it. Asselineau will explain that Gérard was never mad; yet he committed suicide, he hanged himself. You know, at the door of a gin-mill, in a notorious street. Hanged himself! Why did he decide to die in that miserable place, and with a rope around his neck? There are subtle, caressing, ingenious poisons, thanks to which death begins by delight, at least by dreams ... " I said nothing, I dared not speak. "But no, no," he went on, raising his voice, almost shouting now, "it's not true, he didn't kill himself, he didn't, they made a mistake, they lied! No, no, he wasn't mad, he wasn't ill, he didn't kill himself! Did he? You'll tell, you'll tell everyone that he wasn't mad and that he didn't kill himself, promise me to say he didn't kill himself!" I promised everything he asked, trembling in the darkness. He stopped talking. I longed to lie down and get some rest. I didn't move, for fear of bumping into some piece of furniture, and besides, I was waiting for something, I'm not sure what. Suddenly I heard a sob, muffled, choked, as though from a heart breaking under a great burden. And there was only one sob. Fear held me motionless.

I was overcome, I closed my eyes so as not to see the shadow in front of me, in the mirror ...

'When I woke up, Baudelaire was no longer there ...'

(d) 'Boy with cherries'

The theme of hanging had at the time been hideously revived by a dramatic episode, that of the suicide of Alexandre, Edouard Manet's errand-boy, the 'Boy with Cherries' of the Gulbenkian collection, which inspired what is perhaps Baudelaire's blackest page of grotesque humour, 'La Corde' in the *Poèmes en prose*, in which he will pour out his final bitter attack against the crimes of mothers.

Supposedly it is Manet who tells the story, but we have no difficulty in recognizing in the descriptions of this child the features of our little monster :

'In the secluded neighbourhood I live in, and where broad stretches of grass still separate the buildings, I often noticed a child whose ardent and mischievous face attracted me at first sight more than all the other children. He has posed more than once for me, and I have transformed him into now a little gypsy, now an angel, now a mythological Eros. I have given him the vagabond's violin, the Crown of Thorns and the Nails of the Passion, and Cupid's Torch.'

Manet is occasionally surprised by the child's 'strange fits of precocious melancholy', and one day when he had reprimanded the boy for a petty theft, having threatened to send him back to his parents, he returns from a long errand and finds the child has hanged himself,

'his face swollen, and his eyes wide open, with a terrifying fixity'. He cuts him down, 'but even then everything wasn't over; the little monster had used a slender cord which had sunk deeply into his flesh, and now I had to snip at this cord with tiny scissors between two rolls of swollen flesh in order to free his neck.'

16

ENVOI

From his birth to his death.

The fingers opening, what recesses, what resources!

And the 'good *Minet*', who is probably Monselet,

'They call me the *kitten*';

And the sentence about the 'mysterious use' of 'modern stupidity and nonsense ... '

The turn-table of the dream leads down so many tracks!

NOTE

All the words in italics, in the quotations, have been underlined by Baudelaire himself.

SECOND NOTE

Some may consider that, intending to talk about Baudelaire, I have succeeded only in talking about myself. It would certainly mean more to say that it is Baudelaire who was talking about me. He is talking about you.

EDITOR'S NOTE

Quotations from the works of Edgar Allan Poe are given in the form used in the original texts.

SELECTED BIBLIOGRAPHY

A list of the principal works of Michel Butor, with the dates
of their first appearance

PASSAGE DE MILAN (Éditions de Minuit, Paris, 1954)
L'EMPLOI DU TEMPS (Éditions de Minuit, Paris, 1956)
LA MODIFICATION (Éditions de Minuit, Paris, 1957)
LE GÉNIE DU LIEU (Grasset, Paris, 1958)
RÉPERTOIRE I (Éditions de Minuit, Paris, 1960)
DEGRÉS (Gallimard, Paris, 1960)
HISTOIRE EXTRAORDINAIRE (Gallimard, Paris, 1961)
MOBILE (Gallimard, Paris, 1962)
RÉSEAU AÉRIEN (Gallimard, Paris, 1962)
DESCRIPTION DE SAN MARCO (Gallimard, Paris, 1963)
RÉPERTOIRE II (Éditions de Minuit, Paris, 1964)
ILLUSTRATIONS (Gallimard, Paris, 1964)
6.810.000 LITRES D'EAU PAR SECONDE (Gallimard, Paris,
    1965)
PORTRAIT DE L'ARTISTE EN JEUNE SINGE (Gallimard,
    Paris, 1967)
RÉPERTOIRE III (Éditions de Minuit, Paris, 1967)
ESSAIS SUR LES ESSAIS (Gallimard, Paris, 1968)

Principal Translations

SECOND THOUGHTS (LA MODIFICATION), translated by
    Jean Stewart (Faber, London, 1958)
PASSING TIME (L'EMPLOI DU TEMPS), translated by Jean
    Stewart (Faber, London, 1961)
DEGREES (DEGRÉS), translated by Richard Howard
    (Methuen, London, 1962)

THE AUTHOR

Michel Butor was born on September 14th, 1926, at Mons en Baroeul in the north of France, and went to Paris at the age of three. After studies in philosophy at the Sorbonne he led the life of a freelance writer and lecturer. He has taught at universities in France, Egypt, Great Britain (his spell at Manchester resulted in *L'Emploi du Temps*), Greece, Switzerland and the United States. He was awarded the Prix Renaudot for *La Modification* in 1958. Married and father to three daughters, Michel Butor now lives near Paris.

CAPE EDITIONS